PENGUIN BOO

REUNION

Ann Howarth is a Wellington journalist. She attended the
Wellington Polytechnic journalism course in 1979, and
spent her first years in journalism as a reporter on provincial
newspapers. After travelling overseas for two years she
joined the *Dominion* in Wellington, where she worked as
police and then health reporter. After writing this book
she returned to the *Dominion*.

Ann Howarth is adopted, and began searching for her
birth mother in 1979. In 1986 she met her maternal birth
grandmother and other relatives. Her birth mother died of
cancer in 1983, aged forty-two.

Reunion

Ann Howarth

PENGUIN BOOKS

PENGUIN BOOKS

Penguin Books (NZ) Ltd, 182–190 Wairau Road, Auckland 10, New Zealand
Penguin Books Ltd, 27 Wrights Lane, London W8 5TZ, England
Viking Penguin Inc., 40 West 23rd Street, New York, New York 10010, USA
Penguin Books Australia Ltd, 487 Maroondah Highway, Ringwood, Australia 3134
Penguin Books Canada Ltd, 2801 John Street, Markham, Ontario, Canada L3R 1B4

Penguin Books Ltd, Registered Offices: Harmondsworth, Middlesex, England

First published 1988
Copyright © Ann Howarth, 1988
All rights reserved

Typeset by Typocrafters Limited, Auckland
Printed in Australia by Australian Print Group, Maryborough, Vic.

For Jo

CONTENTS

Preference and Acknowledgements 9

Introduction 11

1. *A reflection of myself*: April Anne 15
2. *Like a person from outer space*: Michael 33
3. *On the vicar's doorstep*: Helen 49
4. *Rounding things out a bit*: Julie 63
5. *I couldn't be Maori or Pakeha*: Patricia 74
6. *The opportunity was there*: David 83
7. *A medical history of my own*: Sandy 95
8. *Unreal expectations*: Elizabeth 107
9. *From every point of view*: Gloria 117
10. *Moses in the bullrushes*: Ian 132
11. *Out of wedlock*: Sister Theresa 138
12. *I just started sobbing*: Ruth 147
13. Vetoes 158
14. Birth parents 169
15. Adoptive parents 184
16. Adoption today 189

Appendices 198

PREFACE AND ACKNOWLEDGEMENTS

This book is primarily about *adult* adoptees — in the context of people adopted when they were babies and who grew up with little, if any, knowledge of their origins — who have made contact with one or more of their birth relatives. It has grown out of my personal experience as an adoptee, the suggestion of a friend to write it down, and the need to hear of how other adoptees feel. The case studies were chosen with the help of Social Welfare Department staff, adoption groups and my personal acquaintances, with the aim of providing a representative picture of the experiences of New Zealand adoptees who have actively searched for their birth parents. While it is not a scientifically based random social study, many themes have emerged which are also common to other literature written by both adoption professionals and those personally involved.

'Reunion' is the term commonly used to describe a meeting between an adoptee and her or his birth mother and/or other birth relatives.

The questions foremost in my mind while writing this book were: what percentage of adoptees wish to trace their birth origins, and why? And what is the outcome for those who do search and make contact? But those questions continued to haunt me as I delved further into the subject. None of the research I have read has satisfied my definition of an unbiased study, but all points to the conclusion that many, many adoptees worldwide have not only a curiosity but a deep need to know both the circumstances surrounding their adoption and their genetic background, and that in many, many cases a reunion is an extremely positive experience, not only for the adoptee but also for their birth relatives.

I believe all adult adoptees have the right to a knowledge of their origins. I hope *Reunion* will be of some value to the many thousands of adoptees in New Zealand and elsewhere; their families; and the professionals who set the policies for the future and work within them.

Reunion could never have been written without the love and understanding of both my families, particularly my parents, Alison and Tom, and my grandmother Bid. It would never have been started or completed without the encouragement and support of Chris Harrington and Debra Johanson, Trish Grant, Julie Colquhoun, Lesley Patston, Anita Busby, Tony and Wilma, Sharon and David, and other friends and colleagues.

My very special thanks go to the adoptees who gave generously of their time and energy to share their personal experiences, and whose stories make up most of this book, and the birth mothers and adoptive parents who also shared their views. All the experiences written about are true. However, many of the names, dates, places and some minor details have been changed to protect the identities of the individuals concerned and their families. Any likeness to other people is purely coincidental.

Many thanks go to the groups and individuals who fought for and supported the Adult Adoption Information Bill, and those who later gave of their time, knowledge and encouragement to my writing, particularly some Social Welfare Department staff, adoption groups, and MPs Jonathan Hunt and Fran Wilde.

I would also like to thank the Roy McKenzie Foundation and the Social Welfare Department for their financial assistance.

Ann Howarth

INTRODUCTION

'Who am I?' is a question pondered by many adoptees who have no knowledge of their birth origins. The reflection in the mirror resembles no one they know. Their character, talents, strengths and weaknesses may differ from those of their adoptive family. Are those differences just the normal variations between siblings or are they something more than that? And even if they fit perfectly in their adoptive family, they can never attribute anything about themselves to the natural genetic inheritance of 'normal' people. They are also continually referred to as adopted 'children', whether they are eighteen or eighty, and the term becomes offensive in its implication that they never have the normally expected rights of adulthood.

The questions lead some adoptees to search for their birth mother and for other blood relatives. This is not rejection of their adoptive family, nor a sign of mental instability. It often begins as very ordinary and natural curiosity, developing into a deep need for knowledge. It is a search for self-identity.

Secretive adoption practices have been all too commonly assumed to be the standard, traditional approach, and in the best interests of all parties concerned. But while varying forms of adoption have been practised in different cultures for thousands of years, the severing of all links between birth and adoptive families is in fact very much a twentieth-century Western concept, generally formalised in law to protect adoptees from the stigma of being labelled illegitimate. The theory that total secrecy was in the best interests of all the parties involved became popular in the early 1950s, and added to the perceived need for the secrecy to be maintained. But in more recent years illegitimacy has lost much of its former stigma, and research into contact between adult adoptees and birth relatives points to benefits for all the parties involved in the adoption triangle: a sense of completeness for adoptees, resolution of grief for birth mothers and other relatives, and strengthened adoptive family relationships.

In 1985 New Zealand became one of the world's leaders in the field of adoption when Parliament recognised the rights of both adoptees and birth parents by abandoning the strict secrecy laws. The new legislation, the Adult Adoption Information Act, which came into full force on 1 September 1986, allows both adult adoptees (twenty years and over) and birth parents of adult adoptees the opportunity to make contact with each other, unless a ten-year renewable veto on identifying information has been placed by the other party.

However, the Adult Adoption Information Act was not passed without a lengthy battle. MP Jonathan Hunt began the struggle to open the records in the late 1970s, and over the years was flooded with thousands of letters, with the vast majority in support of abandoning the rule of strict secrecy in adoption. Many of the letters are obviously not the work of organised lobby groups; they are the personal, heartfelt pleas of adoptees and birth parents that the law be changed:

'I have read many horrific suppositions in the media regarding our [adoptees'] origins. Our mothers may have been victims of rape, incest, or have been patients in mental hospitals. All this may be so, but let those of us who need to know, and have the courage to take up our searches, face the trauma as other ordinary people do. I am sure these things do not only apply to adoptees. Let us find and face our heritage, "warts and all", as non-adoptees must. At present we are burdened with being a group of people who are cast into genealogical limbo. Surely society does not want us to be punished for the "sins of our parents" . . . remember we are *adults*, not, as we seem to be continually referred to as, *children* . . .'

'. . . What a marvellous thing it would be for me to be able to give my children and grandchildren the one thing that most people take as a matter of course — a family history. I am not looking for another mother — I have a very gracious one . . .'

In the years leading up to, and following, the new legislation, adult adoptees who had met their birth parents also wrote to Hunt telling him about the experience:

'I am adopted and couldn't have had better parents, but I, like so many adopted children, have suffered the cruel frustration of not being able to trace my birth mother. In May of this year I was able to have the joy of finding my birth mother. It has been a wonderful time for us both and we have received support from my adoptive parents, her children and husband. I only wish I hadn't had to wait till I was twenty-five years old for this to happen, as I feel it has had unnecessary emotional upsets for me and my birth mother. I can only stress that there is room for two mothers and that adoptive parents have nothing to fear, and may in fact have an improved relationship with their children . . .'

'I myself was adopted and was brought up in an extremely happy and supportive environment by my adoptive parents. I have always known that I was adopted and was very relaxed about that situation right throughout my childhood. In the 1970s I became curious about my genetic background and began making attempts to trace my natural parents. My curiosity heightened with the birth of my own son. In him I could see abilities and characteristics that had come from me. In fact I realised that he was the only blood relative that I knew. I wondered where my own abilities and physical characteristics had come from. When the Act came into effect on 1 September 1986 . . . I was eventually able to locate and contact my birth mother . . . I could never have imagined such a positive and welcoming response. The circumstances surrounding my adoption have been fully aired — it was undoubtedly the best course of action at the time. On my mother's part I sense a great unburdening and feeling of relief at being able, after so many years, to tell her family about me. My birth must have been a traumatic experience for her in the unsupportive social climate of the time, and made so much more so by having to remain silent for so long. For my part I feel as though a gap in my past has been filled at last. In no way has this knowledge affected my relationship with my adoptive parents — on the contrary it has cemented it . . .'

Perhaps the impetus in New Zealand for opening records, and the subsequently high application rates, have been more pronounced than in other comparable countries partly because all non-Maori New Zealanders are fairly recent descendants of other cultures, be they neighbouring Pacific Island, continental European, or the common blend of Scottish, Irish and English cultures. Many non-Maori New Zealanders still have relatives living in their 'home' country, and that genealogical-cultural heritage is important to them. But for adoptees such a family tree is, to put it bluntly, a lie. Maori cultural values also place a strong emphasis on family links and blood heritage. In fact, there is no exact Maori word for Pakeha-style adoption because it is a foreign concept, although informal open adoption within extended family groups (where the adoptee grows up knowing the birth parents and other relatives) has been and still is a common practice. New Zealand also likes to see itself as a leader in human rights issues, right from the often-quoted 'first' in giving women the vote. Adoption, too, is an issue of human rights.

ONE

A reflection of myself: April Anne

On 28 July 1983, a forty-two-year-old woman known to her friends and family as Jo died of cancer. In the short weeks leading up to her unexpected death her mother and younger sister attempted to find Jo's daughter, April Anne, born in 1961 and adopted at the age of two weeks.

Three years later, almost to the day, the author learned that Jo was her birth mother. She had started looking for her seven years earlier.

I step out of the taxi hesitantly, late because my car has broken down. There is an elderly woman waiting impatiently at the gate across the road, almost pacing footprints into the path on this warm and sunny winter's day. We look questioningly at each other, both apprehensive yet excited.

She is tiny, petite, her fine hair turned to soft grey at seventy. The years marked into her soft skin show love but also the sorrows and tragedies of life. We are the same height, the same build. I am twenty-five, my hair still golden with youth, skin as yet unlined. We search each other's face for recognition, absorbing the similarities untouched by time. We have never met before but there is no mistake. She is my maternal grandmother; I am her granddaughter. Our eyes are wet as we hug long and gently, holding onto the moment. Inside the house, her sister-in-law's home, we sit closely holding hands while she tells me of the family I have never known. Until this time all I knew about my birth was the date, 25 April 1961, and the place, Wellington. I was adopted at two weeks old.

I can't remember a time of not knowing I was adopted, and there was never shame or prejudice attached to the words. I was never teased about it at school, never ashamed, but as a child I didn't consciously understand what it meant — or did I? The memories have started to come back: I must have been about seven or eight, playing 'dress-ups' by myself. I placed a soft, sea-green, tinkling mobile over my head, the translucent discs falling down my fine long hair. Looking in the mirror, imagining I was really a princess and when I was grown up all would be revealed, the game was no longer make-believe. I wasn't a princess from a far-off foreign land, but nor was I my parents' natural daughter. I quickly placed the 'crown' back in its usual position, the guilt of my realisation flooding over me. The thoughts were placed at the back of my mind, too difficult to deal with at the time.

At eleven I learned that not all New Zealanders were white, Pakeha. But that was easy enough to deal with — my mother was part-Maori, and so was I! I could name my famous Maori ancestors, as could my one Maori classmate. But there was one small problem — no one really believed the small fair-haired girl! I had to explain I was adopted, and there was something slightly uncomfortable about the word.

One of my earliest memories is Dad calling me his 'darling adopted daughter'. I was 'specially chosen' rather than just 'had' like other children. But it's funny how those words always conjure up a picture of a hospital ward, a baby factory, with rows upon rows of perfect little bundles in whiter-than-white baby blankets. Each little bundle was different and distinguishable, each just waiting for the perfect Mummy and Daddy, who had been carefully vetted for their niceness. They would pick out the most angelic little cherub — I guessed I must have been the prettiest little bundle in that room! However, it was also as though each child was created specifically for the purpose of adoption, as though there was nothing which preceded that purpose. And there was a feeling that despite the love and acceptance which surrounded me, I was somehow different and should consider myself lucky to have been chosen — therefore owing my parents more than if I had been born to them.

My life began with formal applications in place of physical conception; a formal Social Welfare Department application in place of a growing pregnancy; a telephone call and drive to the hospital in place of labour and birth. Baby April Anne ceased to exist when Baby Ann Elizabeth was legally and respectably welcomed into the world. Her new parents took her home to celebrate, to begin their new life together as a family, and to forget the past. The woman who felt her grow inside, suffered the pain of birth, even breast-fed her for those first two weeks, went home to her parents to try to forget.

But there is no doubt that the people I call Mum and Dad are my parents. I love them deeply, and I am their daughter in every way but by birth. They loved and cherished their only child from that very first day. My father worked hard to provide for us. My mother fed me, washed me, made sure I did my homework, taught me to cook and sew, and everything she knew about being a woman. They nurtured and encouraged me, worried whenever I stretched the time I was meant to be home, urged me to use my mind, pass exams and be independent in the world. They have passed on to their daughter so much of themselves, and we are a close family. But as each year goes by, the differences also become more apparent.

The questions about my birth origins began forming in my mind as a teenager but they were never voiced at home. Adoption was a taboo subject — like sex, with which of course it is linked. I can't remember ever actually discussing adoption with Mum and Dad when I was a child but the unspoken message was clear: 'Do not ask, just accept.' I sensed not anger, but fear and rejection in what began as simple curiosity. I could not accept that I should just be grateful for a stable and comfortable life and not question my origins. It was a secret, a mystery which I needed to solve to know who I was. Most people can say, 'I have my mother's hair colour' or 'I have my father's nose', 'My talent for art is from my mother's side of the family' or 'I'm stubborn and argumentative like my father'. Were my talents, strengths and weaknesses simply taught, purely environmental influences, or were they inherited? I needed to know to be able to place myself in the world, to understand my potential, and my limits, as a person.

Mum loves to draw her family around her. Sometimes we look through the old family photograph albums, and yes, there is a distinctive look and talents for music and art which link her family through the generations. Perhaps it is more important to them than some families because of the fascinating history of both the Maori and English ancestors, but no matter how much I am included, I am not linked by blood. Everyone else seems to have Great-Aunt or Uncle so-and-so's eyes or nose or shape of face. I don't. Occasionally someone would innocently suggest I looked a little like one of those ancestors in the old black-and-white pictures. I could never see it, perhaps not wanting to. I knew I was different and their comments just added to my curiosity. How I wished I too could look through an old photograph album and see the side of the family I resembled.

At seventeen I secretly went to a couple of adoption support group meetings in the hope of discovering a way to trace my birth mother, who had become the focus of my interest. But it seemed as though everyone else at those meetings had at least some clue on which to base a search, and I stopped going. The adoption group Jigsaw, which runs an informal register for matching up adoptees and birth parents seeking contact with each other, seemed to offer some hope, but the chance seemed so slim, the $15 fee too much out of a $19 a week bursary, their form requesting details so extensive, and so bare when filled out. I never posted it. I also felt guilty for going behind Mum and Dad's backs, and perhaps not quite ready to face what might be revealed.

Later in the year, and at eighteen, I tried the Social Welfare Department, knowing there was virtually no hope of gaining any information. The staff were pleasant but firm in their words that an adoptee's background was confidential. However, one hope was offered — at twenty, non-identifying information about my birth parents, if there was anything on the file, would be available. I waited patiently and returned to the department just a few days after my twentieth birthday. The social worker was surprised by my keenness, but this time the answer was that absolutely no information could be revealed without my adoptive parents' consent in the form of a signature on a poorly printed form. I now feel outrage at that response, but at the time I walked quietly out of the department, scared that even the offer of information with consent would be withdrawn if anyone dared to challenge their authority. Was I an adopted 'child' forever? Would there ever be a time when I was considered responsible for my own actions, did not need parental consent, and was more than just a chattel signed over in a legal contract? Why should a social worker have the power to withhold that tiny amount of inform-ation which could have meant so much — even my birth mother's age and occupation would have told more about the circumstances of my birth than I could ever have guessed.

I rehearsed over and over asking Mum to sign the form, but couldn't put those thoughts into action. I considered forging the signature, even saying my parents were dead, but was too scared of being found out. It seemed the only option was to wait and hope for other possibilities, rather than risk hurting Mum and Dad with the questions they would probably see as a rejection of themselves as parents.

There seemed to be plenty of time, and adoption never domi-nated my life or became an obsession. I worked hard to develop a career base and then made plans to travel overseas. Life was full and exciting, and the questions about my origins faded a little, never forgotten, but filed away for a time in the future when they could be answered. My birth mother was obviously the key to the past. She was the one who had carried me for nine months, given birth, and signed the papers giving up all rights to her daughter. Even just to see a photograph and be told a little about her, or even better meet her briefly, would have satisfied my curiosity. It didn't seem much to ask. She was not Mother in the sense of a parent — I already had a loving Mum — but she gave me life and I was once part of her. There might also be important family medical history lurking behind the closed files.

I thought about the many reasons why she might have chosen adoption for her daughter. I was never angry about it or felt she had abandoned me — perhaps because as a woman I could understand an accidental pregnancy — and believed, or maybe hoped is the true word, that she had little choice in the adoption decision. The social climate of the early 1960s was very different from today's. There was no government benefit for women with young children they could not support alone, and little moral support for an unmarried young woman, as I guessed she had been, with a baby. Her story might not be the one I imagined — I might be the product of rape, incest or prostitution — and whatever the circumstances, she might be against any contact with the grown woman to whom she once gave birth. She might be married with a husband and family who had no idea of my existence, or she might have forgotten the events of many years before — though I found that difficult to believe. I would respect her wishes not to intrude, but knowing even the barest of facts, no matter how unpleasant or distasteful, was preferable to unanswered questions.

I followed my plans to travel overseas, living out of a pack for the best part of two years, and shortly after returning home Mum suddenly brought up the subject of adoption, asking if I was interested in my birth origins. Her words brought immense relief and also great pleasure at being able to talk openly at last. She admitted she would have been reluctant to discuss it in the past but now saw that nothing could change our relationship as mother and daughter. She was right. But her memories of the adoption details were hazy. She thought, but was very unsure, that my birth mother's name was April Farley, though April might have stuck in her mind because that was the month I was born.

What did I do with that information? Nothing. Why? I still don't know. Again, perhaps I wasn't ready — and it seemed wrong to rush into a search based on a name that might be totally incorrect. There was also hope at that time that adoption laws might change to allow adult adoptees and birth parents access to information about each other. As the months passed, it seemed more likely a Bill before Parliament to change the law would succeed, and on the night of 11 September 1985 it was passed.

I read with enthusiasm the following morning's newspaper:

> The Bill making it easier for adult adoptees and birth parents to get information about each other neared the end of a seven-year battle to become law last night.
>   The Adult Adoption Information Bill, sponsored by Govern-

ment junior whip Fran Wilde, was given its third reading after a division of 51–25.

The legislation, initiated seven years ago by Postmaster-General Jonathan Hunt, needs only royal assent to become law.

When the Speaker, Dr Gerard Wall, gave the result of the division there was applause around the chamber.

— *Dominion* 12 September 1985

The Bill was to become active law on 1 September the following year, and I put my faith in the hope it offered. One more year didn't seem long to wait; my birth mother would probably be in her forties, and I would be ready for whatever awaited me. There was a possibility she would place a veto on information about herself, as allowed under the new legislation, but I hoped that if we had anything in common she would not do so. I checked to see exactly how and when to apply for my original birth certificate, which should reveal at least her name and age — enough, I hoped, to trace her.

I now have my original birth certificate and it is as precious as I guessed it would be. My birth name, not my mother's as Mum thought, is April Farley. By coincidence, my original middle name is Anne — my adoptive parents also called me Ann. My birth mother was nineteen and living in Wellington when I was born. Instead of a name for my father, it says, 'No details recorded'. But when the certificate arrived I already knew everything and more that was on it. The time for learning about the past came a couple of months before the new law became active.

It was a Tuesday, about 11 a.m. I was working as a daily reporter on the *Dominion* and had just returned to the office after covering a Wellington Hospital Board committee meeting. The large open-plan newsroom was still in its sleepy morning phase, with most of the desks empty, their occupants out on assignment or working a late shift, the old-fashioned typewriters and telephones still in relative peace. I was sorting through my mail, setting priorities for the day, when my telephone rang. I answered thinking it was a potential story, or even better, a lunch invitation!

'Hello, Eileen Preston from the Social Welfare Department speaking,' the woman's voice said.

'Yes,' I replied, searching for recognition of the name and the work I assumed it was related to.

'This is a personal call . . . can you talk at the moment . . . I'm with the department's adoption section,' the voice said hesitantly.

I knew instantly the context of her call, but it seemed so out of place. More than seven years had passed since I first approached the department in the hope of tracing my birth mother, five years since the last contact, and now there were only a couple of months to wait until adoptees had the right to request information. I could feel my heart beating.

Sensing the hesitancy in my manner, she asked, 'I hope I have the right person . . . you contacted the department some years ago . . . I have some information if you are still interested.'

There was no doubt in my response. I had been waiting for this day for what seemed like most of my life. Eileen asked when I would like to see her — perhaps a time when I wasn't working? The next day was my rostered day off, but as I paused to decide on the time, I found I couldn't wait for even one more day to pass. We arranged to meet at lunch-time, and for the next hour my mind was on nothing else. I was nervous but excitement and curiosity reigned. Eileen arrived on time and we talked privately. It was a long, rambling story, which I found difficult to comprehend and do little more than nod when necessary. It was like one of those silly 'good news, bad news' stories. Eileen began with the good news, but warned all was not perfect.

'Your birth family has been looking for you,' she said. 'Your birth mother, I think she was known as Jo, her sister Elizabeth, and your grandmother wrote to us wanting us to contact you — this was a couple of years ago. Because you had already approached the department, and the unusual circumstances, we tried, but I think you were overseas then?'

I nodded, trying to understand her words, excited by them but at the same time sensing there was something she was obviously having difficulty finding the words for.

'Your grandmother was trying to find you . . . but I have some sad news too . . . you see, Jo died of cancer . . . the family still want to meet you . . .'

I couldn't understand at first what she was saying, thinking she meant my grandmother had died. I was sorry to hear that but the primary interest was my mother. I hardly reacted and probably appeared cold and remote. Then as Eileen continued speaking, telling what little she knew about the family, it began to register. She was talking about my mother, Jo, and it was Jo who had died. My grandmother and aunt had been trying to find me because Jo had cancer and was dying. Perhaps Eileen's words were clear and it was my mind that turned them around in disbelief.

Eventually I asked, almost whispering the question and knowing the inevitable answer, 'My mother, Jo, is dead?'

Eileen replied gently, 'Yes — but her family still want to meet you.'

I felt numb, as if in a different place, a different time. I had considered so many possibilities — but never that my birth mother might not be alive. I didn't know how to feel, how to react, and kept thinking, 'I should be tearful, obviously emotional, feeling and showing grief.' The tears wouldn't come. I had never met this woman, Jo, but she was my mother and I had thought about her since the day the meaning of the word adoption became clear. We were part of each other and I had lost any chance of ever meeting her. Robot-fashion I thanked Eileen, assured her I was all right and would let her know if I traced the family, and wrote down the name and out-of-date address for my aunt. I then put on my coat, picked up my handbag and walked out the door into the lunch-time city rush. Standing at the traffic lights, oblivious to everything around me, I felt alone, a lost little girl, in a way I never had before. Walking quickly, hardly thinking, I moved towards the café friends were lunching at, laughing and joking. I walked in and stood there by the table, speechless and confused, tears beginning to form in my eyes. A close friend and colleague stood up and moved towards me, hugged me and steered me away from the eyes and questions of the others. She knew about the meeting with Eileen, and held me softly while I tried to control the sobs to find the words 'My mother is dead.'

We walked into the street and towards the nearest quiet bar with large gin and tonics. Anita took control while I slumped in the lush navy blue seating. The dimly lit bar was almost empty.

'What happened?' she asked.

'Eileen, the social worker, said my birth mother's family was trying to find me when she was dying of cancer . . . it's almost exactly three years ago. Social Welfare rang the *Herald-Tribune*, where I used to work, and the address I'd given them about five years ago, and they were told I was overseas. No one could've contacted me then . . . I s'pose I would've been in Iran or Turkey, maybe somewhere else around there, I don't think we'd got to Britain then . . . I'm not sure, we were just travelling. She said they didn't contact Mum and Dad because I'd said I couldn't talk to them about it . . . but even Mum and Dad wouldn't have known where I was or how to get in touch with me. Then just the other day the social worker who'd been dealing with it saw my byline in the paper . . . so Eileen called me.

'Jo, my birth mother, apparently died very suddenly and was only in hospital for several weeks. I would've flown straight back here if I'd known . . . I used to wonder sometimes what would happen if Mum or Dad needed to contact me urgently . . . it would've taken weeks to find me. But maybe, in some ways, it's better that I didn't meet her just before she died . . . I don't know . . . I wanted to meet her so much . . . and she wanted to meet me too. Why did it happen then . . .'

Anita listened patiently, supportively, while I went over and over what Eileen had told me and the questions neither of us could answer.

'What do I do now? Eileen said Jo's family still wanted to meet me but she hasn't been able to trace them because the addresses are out of date . . . it's part of our job to trace people . . .'

The obvious place to start was the office, where a wealth of information was at my fingertips in the nationwide telephone books and old electoral rolls — and we both had to get back to work anyway.

I had my aunt's married name and an apparently old address in a provincial city. There was no listing in the current phone book or electoral roll, but luck was on my side — listings in the previous electoral roll suggested she was either divorced or separated from her policeman husband. He couldn't have had a better occupation for my purpose — I checked the office list of police. He was based at the central station, virtually just down the road.

Should I ring? Should I write? What should I do? From what Eileen had said it seemed that I was no secret in the family, and that my approach would be welcomed. I would ring, but couldn't find the courage or think of the right words to say. There was also another phone call to make first — to my adoptive mother. Mum must have wondered what on earth was wrong when I called and only managed to get out a few words of greeting before breaking down and sobbing loudly into the phone. Between sobs I told her what had happened. Her reply was hesitant but supportive, her voice full of love and caring for me, and perhaps a little fear for all of us. I promised to visit soon.

I attempted to concentrate on getting some necessary work out of the way but all I could think of was my aunt's husband, Robin. Thinking carefully about what to say, I finally dialled the familiar police station number and was put straight through. I told him my name, took a deep breath, and plunged in, trying to sound casual and confident while carefully choosing the words.

'I hope I'm right in thinking you are, or were, Elizabeth's husband? I'm ringing as I'm trying to get in touch with her family and I've only got their old address.'

'Who are you?' he asked repeatedly; suspiciously, I thought.

I kept rephrasing the words that I just wanted to contact the family, eventually saying, 'I think I'm related to her family.'

Again he responded, 'Who are you?'

Hoping it wasn't giving too much away, I said hesitantly, 'I think I'm related to Elizabeth's sister, Jo.'

There was a slight pause before he replied. 'I think I know who you are . . . you're Jo's daughter, aren't you?'

'Yes.'

'You know . . .'

'Yes . . . cancer.'

His voice filled with warmth and enthusiasm as he told me the family had been looking for me and would be overjoyed that I had turned up. We met an hour later. Robin picked me up from work, recognised me from across the street, hugged and welcomed me without hesitation. We talked at length over a quiet drink. I hardly knew where to start with the questions, but Robin took the lead. He had known Jo for many years before her death and talked about a woman who celebrated life, was vibrant, talented, intelligent and beautiful. I listened eagerly, trying to absorb every word, every memory, almost overwhelmed by the unexpected warmth and praise of my mother — and the fact that I could never meet her. He also repeated her words spoken shortly before her death, only weeks after learning she had cancer: 'I may have only lived about forty years but I have done as much in that time as many eighty-year-olds.' The same words have been repeated by other relatives.

Robin's memories of Jo told a great deal about her as a woman. He held her in high regard, and I half wondered whether he was my father, although there was no physical resemblance. He sensed those thoughts and brought up the subject before I could ask.

'No, I'm not your father — Jo never really told anyone who was.'

But Robin could tell me that I was conceived when Jo was nineteen, a nursing student in Wellington and away from home for the first time. She was the second-eldest daughter in a large farming family, and gave up nursing to return to the family home after my birth. She married twice, the first time just two years after my birth, but could never have another child. In her late twenties she trained as a teacher and specialised in art. I had three aunts and two uncles, one just two years older than I. A third uncle had been killed in a car accident less than a year earlier. My grandmother was alive and well at seventy, and had remarried after the death of my grandfather. Fears that perhaps I was a dark secret in my birth mother's past were unfounded — the family knew Jo had given up a baby girl, the first grandchild, for adoption.

Robin proved a good starting-point. As I'd guessed, he was separated from my aunt, but he told me the facts without too much embroidery of his own opinions and prejudices. After we'd talked he rang my grandmother and was obviously pleased to be calling with what he knew was good news. There was no reply, but not defeated, he rang around the family and discovered she was in Wellington for a few days! He called the number.

'I guess you're a bit surprised to hear from me . . . but I've got someone here I think you'd like to meet . . . it's Jo's daughter, April, she's right here in the same room.'

Robin passed the phone over. I didn't know what to say and was in tears — but this time tears of happiness — and wasn't alone in that reaction. We spoke briefly, but my only memory of the conversation is that we arranged to meet the next morning.

Sometimes I wonder whether Jo and I would have recognised something in each other had we ever met without knowing we were mother and daughter. I will never know, but there was no doubt in my mind when I met my grandmother who she was. We held each other closely and in the house sat holding hands while we talked, holding on to what we had both discovered. I could have sat there for hours just staring at her! For the first time in my life I was looking at a blood relation, and in a way it was looking at a reflection of myself at seventy. Our facial features are different, mine more like my grandfather's side of the family, but anyone seeing us together would instantly recognise the relationship.

I am very much like Jo in looks; not identical, but obviously her daughter. We have the same colouring, blonde hair with dark brown eyebrows and lashes, and skin that tans easily. She was a little taller than I — but more importantly than physical looks, the picture of Jo that I have gradually pieced together from photographs and memories tells me more about myself than I could ever have imagined. Certainly we are different people, and perhaps I look too hard for similarities and parallels, but at the same time there is too much to simply dismiss as coincidence. Sometimes I have felt as though I am two different people. One is shy and reserved, the other is more assertive, vibrant, ready and willing to take risks in exchange for the experience and excitement — I believe those characteristics are inherited. Jo began training as a nurse; I was accepted for nursing at sixteen and decided against attending the course. She worked briefly as a newspaper photographer; I have worked as a newspaper reporter and have a keen interest in photography. She was also a talented clothing designer. My grandmother says that once Jo learnt to sew she began designing and would virtually lay material on the floor and cut without a pattern. I was stunned — Mum, who taught me to sew using patterns, long ago gave up on my methods, which were the same as Jo's. I followed my intuition and instincts. Surely something like that cannot be inherited — or can it?

I stared and stared at those first photographs of Jo, fascinated by the physical image, but what hit me most looking through the album she had made up was that it reflected not only her life but in many ways mine also. It was all there, from toddler to mature woman. The chubby little four-year-old, so much like the one in my old photograph album, school reports with the familiar comments: 'A pleasing pupil . . . good work . . . but could probably do better.' Her moves from town to town, black-and-white photographs she had taken and printed, parties where she had a glass of wine in one hand and a man on the other arm — a different one for each segment of her life! There was a four-leaf clover pressed between the pages, perhaps the obvious place to preserve it, but there is also one carefully placed in the album I kept as a teenager!

I have pored over and over Jo's photographs, not only trying to bring her alive in my mind, but also looking for a clue to the identity of my father. There is one page with two photos dated 1960, the year I was conceived. One is of Jo and Michael, a 'sailor', the other Jo and Mike, a 'copper'. My grandmother suspects Mike is my father, but he is tall and dark, with quite different looks from mine. Jo's first husband has told me a different story. He says she talked a great deal about her daughter, April. When they found she could not have another child they considered trying to get me back, but decided, quite correctly I believe, it would be unfair to even attempt it. I would have been about three years old. Jo told him my father was a red-headed hairdresser who went to Australia when told she was pregnant. The description fits with the skimpy background information the Department of Social Welfare finally made available, at my specific request, while I was writing this book. The staff member who gave me a copy did not realise I had no knowledge of the following form which they had prepared — but would not make available without parental consent — when I requested the information as a twenty-year-old. It is not even addressed to me.

DETAILS ABOUT YOUR CHILD

Name: Ann Elizabeth Howarth
Date of birth: 25 April 1961   *Sex*: Female   *Place*: Alexandra
Weight: 7 lb   *Delivery*: Not known
Description at birth: Not known   *Registered*: Wellington
Progress before placement: Made excellent progress under Plunket supervision
Date of placement: 9 May 1961 by Matron from Alexandra

PERSONAL DETAILS

Mother: Single	*Father*
Age: 19 years *Race*: European	*Age*: Not known *Race*: European
Occupation: Clerk, Army Headquarters	*Occupation*: Barber
Health: Always good health	*Health*: Not known
Education: 3 years post primary. School Certificate	*Education*: Not known
Intelligence: Intelligent	*Intelligence*: Intelligent
Religious denomination: Presbyterian	*Religious denomination*: Not known
Personality: Well spoken. A very good balanced personality	*Personality*: Not known
Interests: Not known	*Interests*: Not known
Family History: Family relationship good. Second in a family of seven. Her parents aware of her situation	*Family History*: Not known
Description: 5′ 5½″ slight build. Fair complexion. Well groomed. Attractive appearance	*Description*: Auburn hair. Green eyes

Additional comments by officer: A superior girl. Intelligent boy P.P.
Natural mother's reason for adoption: Unable to support a child
Interim order: 14 June 1961
Final order: 19 February 1962

There may be further details on my full file, which has been 'temporarily lost' by the department. But even if the file is found and there is a name for my father, there is no guarantee that it is correct. And while I am aware of this, the department's policy is not to release the information — although they will trace him for me and ask if he would be willing to meet me. Would I search for him if I knew his name? Yes; there is still part of me missing. I am not angry with him — I know virtually nothing about the circumstances of my conception, whether my mother loved or hated him, or how he felt, and it is all in the past now anyway. But from the little I do know, presuming it is correct, which it may not be, it seems likely he will not want to know me — but then he might. There might also be other daughters and sons, my half-siblings. I would not confront him suddenly, purposefully interfere in his life, or demand he be a father to me — I already have a father. His only part in my life was apparently his sexual pleasure, but in that he contributed part of himself, his genetic history, to my being — and I have a right to knowledge of that history. All I want is a little information, and if he is willing, maybe to meet and get to know him — if he is still living.

I have been welcomed into Jo's family and I rejoice in that, though this is mixed with the emotions of grief over her death. In some ways it is as though I grew up in another country and then travelled many miles to meet relations — an exciting time for any family. I felt nervous to begin with, meeting everyone, trying to work out who was who, where I fitted in, and what they would think of my sudden appearance. Again, we all stared at each other, absorbing the physical similarities. I realised there was no need for me to be nervous, no need for pretences as to who I was, all I had to do was relax and be myself in a way I had never been able to do before. For the first time in my life I didn't feel the odd one out at a large family gathering. I was a little different, a little nervous, but I also felt a new inner security in the knowledge that I was part of this family by birth.

The first family photograph I saw was of Jo's youngest brother, only two years older than I. We look like brother and sister. When we met we went for a long walk in the rain to the river by which Jo had loved to spend time. Walking on the family farm, following the river bank, I had this eerie feeling of having come home. It seemed incredibly natural to be there. I was with a man I hardly knew but, if circumstances had been different, would have grown up with, played with almost as brother and sister.

Knowing my birth family and having ongoing contact with grandmother, aunts, uncles and cousins does not detract from my adoptive family; I have two families now. Love is not a finite emotion with a limited quantity which has to be spread more thinly with each new relationship. There is no doubt in my mind that the man and woman who brought me up are my parents. They are Mum and Dad, their family is my family, and they are the people I will always go to in times of joy or crisis. Mum understands but it has been difficult for Dad. I saw them the day after I met my grandmother, Mum having told Dad what had happened. He was uncomfortable, I think only accepting my contact with birth relatives because Jo was not alive. It is all out in the open now, but even so, adoption is not a subject we can discuss comfortably. Our opinions differ enormously but in some ways we are now closer than before, and he has been incredibly supportive of my writing this book. He was, and still is, opposed to the Adult Adoption Information Act, and try as I can, I cannot forget his sharp mind and tongue arguing that allowing adult adoptees and birth parents access to information about each other is breaking a confidential legal contract. Technically he is correct — the Act is a retrospective law change — but as the third party in that contract, the party whose interests were meant to be paramount, I had no say and was presumed never to desire or be entitled to an opinion. I am not a chattel to be bargained over and never was. I am also not an adopted 'child' any more. As an adult, I believe adoptees do have at least the moral right to ask questions about their origins — and the right and courtesy of at least some honest answers.

I have been cheated by that law, and concept, of confidentiality. It has stolen from me every possible chance of meeting my birth mother, and probably also my birth father. It secured my legal rights as the legitimate daughter of my adoptive parents and a secure family upbringing, and has given me two parents I love dearly and who can never be replaced. But at the same time it has robbed both me and Jo of something priceless.

Many months after writing the above words, I received a letter from Jo's second husband. It said:

'. . . I only wish that she had gone through with her intention of trying to contact you while the chance was there. She always wondered what had become of you, [your] likes, dislikes and life in general.

'She was a wonderful person and I am sure you would have gotten along with her — she always worried that you would have been angry, which I think is why she never went through with contacting you.'

How I wish we could have met, not just for my sake I realise now, but for her sake too.

TWO

Like a person from outer space: Mike

Born in 1960, Mike grew up knowing he and his younger brothers and sister were adopted. Shortly after the Adult Adoption Information Act came into effect, Mike applied for his original birth certificate, received it and traced his birth mother to Perth, Australia. They have since met and formed a close relationship.

On the surface Mike is the average middle-class New Zealander, successful in his career and marriage. He is a sensitive and caring man, a stable husband and loving father to the couple's two little boys. He had a happy childhood and loving parents, with whom he feels a close bond and sees regularly. But he says there have been times when he felt as though he arrived on this planet from outer space — because he is adopted.

'I've known I arrived in the family by adoption for as long as I can remember,' he says. 'I have one memory of standing at the sink, I'm sure it was pre-school, Mum was doing the dishes and telling me something about it.

'She said: "You didn't grow in Mummy's tummy, you grew in another lady's tummy. We don't know very much about it but we know she loved you very much but she couldn't keep you, and you came into this family. We picked you out of all the babies and we love you very much."

'The subject didn't come up very often,' Mike says, 'maybe once a year, but if it did and we had questions, they were always answered. I remember getting a bit upset about it when I was about twelve years old, maybe it was adolescence starting, but that was about the only time I thought about it very much until a couple of years ago when watching my own children grow up.

It was really apparent how the two boys had different characteristics from Linda, my wife, and I, and that sort of set my mind going. Daniel, he's three and very much like me, he's sort of got a double personality and is an emotional person. Mum says, "He's just like you at that age — you were a little hound!" She also says that when we were very young she had this idea that the babies she got were like blanks that she could programme and give them personal characteristics through her and the environment we grew up in. Now she is firmly of the view that basic personality is there at birth, because the four of us, all adopted, are all very different people. We get on pretty well; we're just like a normal family except that in some families there's a common theme running through and you'd never get anything like that in my family.'

The only sibling interested in his birth origins, Mike watched the progress of the Adult Adoption Information Bill and shortly after it became active legislation applied for his original birth certificate. He received it promptly and discovered his original name had been Simon Keith Harrison. His birth mother's name, at seventeen, was Katherine Jane Harrison. The Department of Social Welfare also provided background information which included bare details of both birth parents' ages, occupations, education, interests and a brief physical description. The sparse two pages concluded with the comments:

> Your mother's parents were aware of the pregnancy. Your birth father had helped financially throughout and after the pregnancy. The couple planned to marry when they were older but felt it was not fair to you to keep you unless they were married.

In six weeks Mike had traced his birth mother to what appeared to be a current address in Perth, Australia. Two days later he posted this letter, using a Perth solicitor as an intermediary:

> Dear Katherine,
> This letter is being conveyed to you via the solicitor, Ms Armstrong, so that your personal privacy will be protected.
>   My name is Michael Anthony Carter (Mike). I am writing to you in the hope that this letter will be welcome. I was born on 27 August 1960, in Auckland, New Zealand, to Katherine Jane

Harrison. My registered name at birth was Simon Keith Harrison. I was adopted out at birth. I believe you are my birth mother. I know your name because I obtained a copy of my original birth certificate under the New Zealand Adult Adoption Information Act. A copy is enclosed.

I have traced you primarily through your father, James McDonald Harrison. I have written how I located you later on in this letter. I am approaching you because I would like very much to know that you are there and know of me, and I of you. In this letter I have endeavoured to present myself to you so that you will see that I mean no threat to you, and that I do not seek in any way to disturb the life that you have and the things that have happened to you over the years. I know you are married and believe you have new children of your own, and that you will be concerned to protect them and their lives from disturbance. I do not know if your husband knows of my existence. I do not seek to change any of this.

There are probably many traumatic memories of the past associated with the adoption. I know that you will wonder whether the past should be re-opened. Perhaps you will wonder whether it would be better for all if these things were allowed to remain undisturbed. Before I applied for the details of you I had similar thoughts. I wanted to know you and about my beginnings but did not know what sort of feelings and emotions I would arouse if I went ahead. When I did get the certificate I just looked at it for a time. It took me a while to adjust to the things it told me, and I expect your reactions to this letter will be similar. I hope that you will not dwell too much on the negative aspects of the adoption, however. We should not forget about the good and positive things that could come from our making contact. Perhaps you have wondered at times about what happened to the child you had. Perhaps you have had feelings of uncertainty. I hope that I can show you that you did the right thing for me. I am grateful for the chance you gave me and for your bringing me into the world. I have no 'hang-ups' about the fact that I am adopted. I do not seek to reverse the past.

For my part I sometimes feel like a person who arrived from outer space. I know nothing of my background and how I got here. I have generally been happy to accept the family background that I inherited from my adoptive parents. Within

myself, however, I know that this is a fact that has very much
been 'grafted on'. Having children of my own has made me
realise what I don't know. Their personalities are very much
derived from mine. I know that my beginnings may not be all
rosy. Circumstances that give rise to an adoption will always be
difficult. I know that you may not wish to address the question
of my birth father, and I can accept that. I would rather know
about you only than know nothing at all.

So that you will know something about me I have written
some things below. Some photographs of myself and my wife
and children are enclosed. There is also one of me as a child.

I grew up the eldest in a family of four children. I have two
younger brothers and a younger sister, and we all started life as
adopted. My adoptive mother had difficulties with her own
pregnancies and she and my adoptive father decided to adopt.
Our becoming their family in this way gave them great happiness, and like most lucky parents they continue to watch their
children maturing as adults and to enjoy the 'fruits of their
labours'. One of my brothers is engaged and my sister has been
married for two years, and another grandchild is expected. My
parents do not feel challenged by my approaching you. They are
supportive. My mother says she feels grateful to you for giving
them a chance to have a family.

From an early age we knew we were adopted, and I do not
think that it made any difference to us as children. The
upbringing that we had would not have been different had we
arrived on the scene by direct birth. It was entirely normal.

I grew up and now live in Auckland. I went to a local kinder-
garten and then to a convent school. At twelve I went to a
Catholic college, which I left after the sixth form. At school I
played rugby and then soccer, and later cricket, but it would
definitely not be true to say that I displayed any sporting
prowess! I also liked sailing. Academically I was above average
but I don't regard myself as any great brain. I think I am what's
described as 'a bit of a plodder'!

After school I went to work for the Inland Revenue Department. I passed accounting exams, studying part time, and then
did more study in that area. I took a job with a firm of chartered
accountants and passed my final exams when I was twenty-
three. I am now a partner in the firm and this seems to be the
career into which I have settled.

I married in 1980. My wife's name is Linda and we have two boys, Alex and Daniel, aged five and three. A couple of years ago we bought a house in an Auckland suburb and since then I have spent most of my spare time painting and so forth! Next year we plan to live in the UK for a year. I have been to Australia, and Perth incidentally is my favourite city. Last year we had a month in the UK.

You may wish to know how I found you. It is an interesting story, and it was not easy. With the birth certificate, I did a marriage search on you (in New Zealand). I located nothing between 1961 and 1972. I obtained your birth records and they gave me your parents' names and address at the time of your birth. I subsequently located your father and your stepmother at Rotorua at the time of my birth through old electoral rolls. I went to the cemetery at Rotorua and saw your father's grave. With the date of death, I obtained the death notice from the Rotorua newspaper — that gave me your married name and that you lived in Perth. (It also told me that you were alive!) For a time during the search I thought you were a nun. I also saw a Simon Harrison living in Auckland and before I made the Rotorua connection, thought this might be your father. I also talked to a Sister who was the Catholic Social Services counsellor who arranged the adoption.

I hope that you will feel able to reply to this letter. I know that the adoption may well be something very much of the past for you. In a way it is for me too. Its primary effect on my life, in seeing me cared for and giving me a family, is also largely in the past. Now that these aspects are over I hope that we can go a step further. If you need time to sort things out perhaps you could advise the solicitor so I will know what is happening. If you are unable to write for some reason, perhaps you could let her know. If things are such that you do not want to communicate with me, it would be helpful if you could give her some idea of the reason.

Mike

'It was very carefully worded,' Mike says, reflecting back six months. 'I didn't send it directly to her home address because I didn't know whether her husband was my father or not, and he might not have known about me, so I didn't want to put my foot in it from her point of view right from the start, and you never know who in a family opens mail. Most people leave other people's, but it's not inconceivable that a husband could open a wife's mail, and a letter coming from New Zealand to Australia could raise "oh what was that?" Not like a bill or something. So I got in contact with a solicitor in Perth, a lady solicitor, and sent it to her and the phone number. I wanted to make sure that Kate had the option of reading the letter and making a decision without other people in her family knowing.'

The solicitor rang Kate and said, 'I have received a confidential letter addressed to you which you may wish to collect personally. You may also wish to read the contents before mentioning anything about this telephone call to your husband.'

Mike's birth mother replied, 'Is one of my children in trouble?'

'No,' the solicitor said.

'Um — is it anything to do with an adoption in New Zealand in 1960?'

'That's right.'

'Oh . . . could you just put it in the mail to me? We live about an hour's drive out of the city and it's okay to send it here, my husband knows all about it.'

Mike received a brief note from the solicitor a few days later informing him that his letter had been posted to his birth mother at her request. Two days later another letter arrived from Perth:

Dear Mike,

Thanks for writing to me and sharing your thoughts and feelings. I appreciated your honesty and sensitivity. I am in a mild state of shock to be in touch with you. I must have read and re-read your words at least a dozen times. It's all a bit much to take all at once, you and your story bringing me up to date with your life, your wife and the two boys. When I received the phone call from Ms Armstrong I was a little confused, but then I realised it could be you wanting to contact me. I really wasn't surprised. I have often wondered if you would. At times I have wondered and questioned — who, how and what is that first-born child of mine? Thanks for having the courage. I wouldn't have made an attempt myself, I guess mainly so as not to intrude into another family, and also not believing I had any right to. At the time of the adoption I was told a little about your parents, mainly that they were desperate to have a child, that they were financially secure, were Catholic, and you were to be the eldest in their family. I trusted in the advice of the Catholic Social Services and the nun handling it; somehow there didn't seem to be any option. I never felt very much part of the decision. But after all this time it's comforting to know you were loved and cared for within your family.

The most amazing thing is to bring you into the present, to find out your identity, to know your name. It makes you a real person. For years I have carried with me my memories of that period and as the years passed I felt as if you were drifting away. I remember you as a tiny baby, but common sense reminded me you were growing through your childhood, teens and into adulthood. I couldn't relate to that. I could only try and imagine, knowing that's all it was, my imagination. So to receive your letter with the photos is just almost too much. I can't really put it all into words that would make sense, only to say the feelings are many but joy is pretty strong. To actually read your words written personally by you, Mike, to learn of Linda and your sons. I can't digest it all in one bit but I'm working on it. No resentments, no hang-ups, as you say in your letter, you seem to have made the best of it. I have no doubt that your parents truly deserve to reap the rewards of their labours.

I was disappointed to notice on your birth certificate that your father's name was missing. I specifically asked at the time that his name be included. The reason I wanted his name along with my own was as your natural parents I wanted to leave you with something of both of us for you to carry into the future. Any material gift was not allowed, it had to be a final parting. Your father's name is Simon Keith, so you can see where your name came from. I can remember the tender and proud moments he and I shared discussing you, your birth and your name. To us, giving you our own names meant so much as it was the only thing we could give you. Looking at your photo, the present-day one, and reading your letter, I would say you are very much your father's son. In my eyes you look like him and have the same build, but his hair wasn't as dark as yours. Simon was, when I knew him, a quiet, caring, sensitive and serious boy, who had a warm sense of humour, and once he got to know people his personality became more relaxed. He played soccer and a little bit of cricket but like you didn't set the team on fire. He was intelligent and mature for his age. He was around 5 feet 11 inches tall, and lean. He worked in the Bank of New Zealand.

We had been going together for about eighteen months when you were born, and in actual fact wanted to marry when we knew our child was conceived, but the 'parent and priest' generation thought otherwise. However, Simon supported me all through my pregnancy and, when I had to leave Rotorua to live in Auckland about four months before you were born, he drove me up and settled me in. He was very, very supportive both emotionally and financially before, during and after your birth. I felt really sad to see his name missing from your birth certificate. We continued our relationship for about another twelve or eighteen months after your birth but it wasn't to be. I actually saw him about four years ago. I was at Christchurch Airport, leaving to fly back home, when I spotted him in the crowd. He was with a lady and two young girls, who I presumed were his family. I never spoke or showed any sign of recognition (which to this day I have regretted), mainly because I didn't know how to handle it, and by the time I got my thoughts back in control the opportunity had passed.

Now to tell you a little of my life and where it's gone. I married a fellow Kiwi, Steve Hopkins, in Perth in '63. Steve and I have a very happy and close relationship and I reckon he's a great guy. He already knew of your existence and the circumstances so I was immediately able to shared it all with him. We both chuckled over your thinking I might be a nun! Heaven forbid — with due respect. But no, Mike, I couldn't possibly have entered the convent and I'm sure they wouldn't have wanted me. Steve read your letter and encouraged me to reply, he said more for your sake than mine, as he believed you obviously needed to have some knowledge of your beginnings. At this stage he is protective of me and our children and is reluctant to share you with them. We have five children — none of them has married yet.

I work part time and enjoy my job. It's hard to do a pen sketch of oneself, but I guess I can say I'm outgoing, practical, think a lot, normally a happy person with a positive attitude to life. I like doing things with my hands, enjoy most musical styles, enjoy reading and have a deep and personal faith. I left school at the end of the fifth form and worked as a clerk until I left to come to Aussie. I have made several trips back to New Zealand, in fact twice in '85 when Dad was ill and then for his funeral. My dad was a beaut man, a really good and strong person with a very extroverted style and a great sense of humour. He had a real twinkle in his eyes. I don't remember anything of my mother. She died suddenly when I was very young but I would often look at her photos and ponder. Steve and I, and the three younger boys, spent a month in New Zealand over the last December-January period so as to give them our experience of family and also for them to see and feel their Kiwi heritage. Funnily enough, Mike, we visited Dad's grave on the fifth of January so, judging by the date of issue on the birth certificate, you wouldn't have been far behind!

I truly welcome contact with you, Mike, never doubt that, and just to read your thanks and affirmation regarding the decision surrounding your birth means so much. It gives me good feelings and a sense of relief and freedom as I never felt comfortable about the adoption. My way of coping was to tuck it away in the 'corners of my mind' and now to be able to open the lid and be free to talk, to remember, to love and to feel good about myself and about it all is your gift to me. To read your words 'you did the right thing for me. I am grateful for the chance you gave me and for bringing me into the world.' Thanks, Mike — only you can say that to me. As I write, my thoughts return to your father, Simon; he also gave you a chance and he stuck by both of us. I hope this letter can help you to come in a little closer from those 'outer space' feelings. I look forward to further contact and eventually to meeting with you and Linda plus the boys.

Love and God bless you, Mike, and your family.

Kate

After so much caution Mike was thrilled with the response. 'I was at work when Linda rang up about three o'clock to say there was a letter from Perth. I didn't come home early but I didn't get much work done either! I thought it was a really good letter. I s'pose being basically white and middle class you sort of have this expectation that's what will be on the other side, though that's really an unreal expectation. But she was basically much the same. There were photographs of her and her husband and family, and

I felt that she communicated really well. I searched for a likeness in the photos but couldn't see any striking resemblance, though other people say we look alike.

'I read the letter over and over, and wrote back about a week later. I wasn't sure what I was going to do now, how I wanted things to go — it all seemed to become very shaky. We corresponded every few weeks or so, and then got on the phone. I rang up the first time, but she'd said she wanted me to. I felt that, from the point of my initiating things up to the time that I wrote, I'd been calling the shots, but from then on I was very conscious that Kate started to play the leading role. She was the first one to bring up the question of a meeting and somebody going across the Tasman. But trying to arrange that caused a fundamental disagreement — she wanted me to go over there and stay at the house, but with her three younger children not knowing who I was. I really wanted to go over there, but I just didn't think that was right. There was about a week's silence where I thought it had all gone wrong. I'd felt that up to that point we had been really honest and open and I didn't want to change that. It's a very emotional thing where people aren't really thinking straight or being very rational. Anyway, we sorted it out and she came over here for about eight days. [About two months after the first letters.]

'Linda and I went to meet her at the airport, but in the car on the way there it was, "I want to go home, what am I going to do, what am I going to say?" It was just such a big thing. I wanted to keep going, it was just that at the same time I was very nervous about it. I s'pose I was scared really. I was a wimp! We got to the airport and when she came through the door I thought, well I'm not going to shake her hand, I'm going to give her a hug, even though this woman in many respects is still a stranger, I want to make her feel welcome. She'd gone through the birth on a tape and said that it was a very physical thing for her and she just wanted to hug me. I was sort of feeling that way, but she could link back to this baby at birth, whereas I had nothing to link back to. Anyway, when she arrived we hugged but she was like a cold fish — I think she put one arm round me and we got talking about the weather and what the flight was like and all that. It continued on like that until the second night, when she finally sort of broke through it all.'

Linda had gone to bed and Mike and Kate were sitting in the lounge chatting.

'Look, it's not working,' Kate said. 'If it's going to be like this I may as well go home.'

Mike reacted angrily at first. 'What the hell do you expect . . . you can't expect too much all at once.' Then apologising, 'No, I'm sorry, you're right, we're not really communicating.'

'Come and sit next to me . . . I want to hold your hand,' Kate said.

'She basically wanted to cut through all the crap and really communicate,' Mike says now, 'and from that point we became really in touch with each other in a way that was very close. The only other people I have become that close to are my wife and my adoptive mother. I know now that she had just been so emotionally wound up by it all that she was just trying to keep herself calm and the end result was maybe she had overdone it.

'This period of a few hours of very physical closeness seemed to facilitate talking about how we really felt. I admitted that I was really nervous that she wouldn't like me and would go away. She said she would have loved me no matter who I was because I was her child. She'd kept writing that I was very much like my father — I knew she'd finished the relationship with him and I think my fear was that if I was like him, and she had become bored with him and terminated the relationship, she would find the same thing happening with me. She said that was really dumb and wasn't the case. We also went back over the birth. I didn't realise that there were a whole lot of things for her that didn't really involve me to a very large extent — like a whole lot of feelings about how she has handled giving up this child over the years and the birth. I know she's going through dealing with those things now and she's well on the way. We just talked about those sorts of things and had a few hugs.'

Hesitantly, Mike also adds, 'It had sexual overtones — I don't say I'm sexually attracted to her, it's just that normally being close to a female there's that there as well. I found it quite hard to handle. I didn't actually feel that way, but I felt I shouldn't be hugging this person, or something like that. Even before that my feelings about Kate and what was happening had become very intense, and I thought, this is wrong, I'm getting it all out of proportion, I've got to stop. But my counsellor said it was quite common and I shouldn't worry about it. She made the parallel that it was like falling in love — and that's the way I felt. I've also learnt subsequently that's the way Kate was feeling too. It was such a rapid build-up of intense emotional feeling I'd never expected. I was totally wrong on every count in the way I thought I'd feel; in every case it was just a hell of a lot stronger. I've got over that now. I still have very strong feelings towards her but now I can let other people into my life too.

'We drove down to Rotorua the next day, where Kate had grown up, and it brought back all the memories for her. We walked, arm in arm most of the time, round town and to the bank where Simon worked and where they had lunch and talked about how it was going to be when they were married and about the house they hoped to buy. She told me the story of how she'd become pregnant and the attitude of her parents and Simon's parents. We went to his house — they don't live there anymore — and she said, "See that window there? That was the lounge where my parents came in to talk to Simon's parents when I was four months pregnant with you. His mother went berserk and said, 'How can you do this to my son?' We wanted to get married. My father went along with it, he was a very strict Catholic, and thought marriage was the answer. But Simon's mother said no way was she having that."

'I think Simon's mother was right,' Mike says. 'I don't feel any resentment that they adopted me out. Kate has some regrets, but they would have been kidding themselves if they thought it would have worked out. They were very young, and I don't think she's being realistic. She's also making the assumption that I would be the same person as I am now had I been brought up by her and Simon, and chances are, without meaning to be rude, that if they'd got married at seventeen and eighteen it could well have been a broken home and I would have been a delinquent!'

Mike would very much like to meet his birth father, Simon, who lives in Nelson. Shortly after making the initial contact with Kate, he wrote:

Dear Simon,
This letter has been delivered to you via the Social Welfare counsellor so that your confidentiality will be protected.

My name is Michael Anthony Carter (Mike). I was born on 27 August 1960, in Auckland, to Katherine Jane Harrison and my registered names at birth were Simon Keith. I was adopted out at birth. I enclose a copy of my original birth certificate, which I obtained under the Adult Adoption Information Act. The records of Catholic Social Services from 1960, which I had access to confidentially, show you as my birth father. I also obtained some other information from the Department of Social Welfare files which were made available to me, and that is enclosed (Social Welfare do not release parents' names who are not registered).

I am writing to you because I would like for us to make some contact, or at least to know of each other, and while I appreciate that it may take some consideration, I hope that ultimately this letter will be welcome. I hope also that you will see that I do not seek to disturb your life or that of your wife or family, who I appreciate may not be aware of the situation. I should also say that I am not seeking a substitute parent and do not seek to reverse the past.

The pregnancy and adoption are probably parts of something that is long in the past for you. I can understand that they may be things that you are reluctant to recall. Circumstances that give rise to an adoption will never be easy. I know little of the relationship that existed at the time, but I do know that you assisted financially. I do not seek to press you to discuss the past. I have no 'hang-ups' about the adoption and am happy to leave things as they are. At present, however, there is a connection between you and me and, all other things being equal and so long as it is possible without causing difficulty, I would like to come to know you a little. Some of the little details I do know of you suggest that in some respects you may be quite similar to me.

I have written a little about myself below, and a photograph and one of my wife and children are enclosed . . .

When I received my original birth certificate and the other information I have, it took me a time to start to adjust to what it told me, and I expect your reactions to this letter will be the same. I hope that you will be able to reply or that we will be able to meet. If I hear nothing I will at least know that you know of me, and I would be happy for you to contact me in some future year.

Mike

Simon met and spoke with the social worker for about half an hour. He freely admitted being Mike's father, hesitantly accepted the letter, but three months later he had still not replied.

'My initial reaction is to feel annoyed,' Mike says, 'but then I think it's immature to feel that way. I went into it knowing I might not get a reply, and you've got to tell yourself you can handle that. The difficult part is that I know he's alive, I know he's there. He's in the phone book, his work is in the phone book, even some friends went to Nelson on holiday and sent a photo of them standing by the sign outside this guy's office. The opportunity came for me to go to Nelson in connection with work recently, and I wasn't that happy about it — it fell through and I was quite pleased. I don't think I would have spied on him or confronted him, but the temptation would have been there. I'd have been preoccupied and wouldn't have been much good at my work. I feel annoyed that he's just brushing it off — he's my father and yet he's trying to fend it off. I can see a side of me that would do that and yet I'd say that's immature, spineless. But the more I think about it, the more I think there's probably a very good reason — chances are he never told his wife, which would be very difficult, and I've just got to assume it's something like that. It's not a big problem to me, but now that things with Kate are pretty normal I've started to think more about him.'

Mike is still hoping for a response and weighing up whether to make another approach through the social worker.

'Somehow it seems acceptable for a female adoptee to have some special relationship with her birth mother, opposed to her father,' he says, 'but it doesn't seem quite so acceptable for the

male adoptee to want some sort of relationship with his father —
yet because he is my father, I feel very much a need to know him.

'When I first applied for my original birth certificate my attitude
was that if I found nothing my whole life wouldn't come crashing
down around me. I was nervous to find there might be a veto
— I don't say I would have become an emotional wreck as a
result, but that's what I was most nervous about. I just thought
that it might be possible to meet up with this person or people
without it causing them a whole lot of hassles, or me a whole lot
of hassles, and that would be a really positive result. I felt that
if it was going to cause a lot of trouble for people on either side
it wouldn't be worth it. Keeping people happy was more
important than my desire to know, but I feel a little bit differently
now. Once I'd made the contact and found that it was all real,
suddenly the significance and the emotional things just blew up.
Even though that's gone down a bit, it's a far more important
thing than I thought it would be. My attitude now, not having
heard back from my father, is that I think he still has some
residual responsibility to me. You can't discharge all your responsibilities by adoption or a piece of paper. In law you do, but in
a moral sense there's something there. I don't want to wreck his
life, and I still wouldn't try to upset it in any way, but maybe
what responsibility he does have means that it's okay for him to
put up with a little bit of hassle. Maybe it does disturb him a bit
but I feel he has some obligation. Just a knee-jerk pushing it away
— I don't think that's enough. Any birth parent has an obligation to think about it and make an informed decision. If they are
not able to make contact, if they can't handle it emotionally
because they haven't told their spouse or whatever, at least they
should think about it.'

But despite the disappointing silence from Mike's father, contact
with his birth mother has been an overwhelmingly positive
experience. He describes it as 'the major event of the year for
both Linda and I, the major event since our children were born.

'It's made me feel more sort of balanced somehow, happier
about who I am. I can't put a finger on exactly why, but you
know the story and you just feel more stable, like you've got your
feet more on the ground than you did before. For me it's very

much a personality thing, because I've always been aware that
my personality in some respects is a little bit different from the
norm — and then you find a whole bunch of people who are like
that and you can see where you got that from, suddenly you can
fit it. It makes you feel a lot better about who you are.'·

Six months later Mike received a warm and apologetic letter from
his birth father, and the two men, who have much in common
apart from the fact that they are father and son, have since met
twice and are beginning to form a close friendship. As Mike had
guessed, his father had never told his wife about his eldest son.
But with the secret now out in the open, Mike has been welcomed into the family. Kate has also told her other children the
reason for her unexpected visit to New Zealand and they have
happily accepted another brother. Mike's adoptive family have
also met members of his birth family.

THREE

On the vicar's doorstep: Helen

Born in 1921, Helen was about twelve years old when she found out she was adopted. On the same day she also learned that no one knew who her birth parents were — she had been left on a vicar's doorstep without any clue to her identity. Helen began the seemingly impossible search for birth relatives shortly after the Adult Adoption Information Act came into force in 1986.

On the night of 4 November 1921, the vicar of Opawa's Anglican church joined his wife and eldest sons in their front lounge for a cup of tea before retiring to his bed. It was late and their youngest children had long been tucked up when Reverend Williams thought he heard a child's muffled cry. He listened intently, but all was quiet — then again came the same muffled sound.

'Is that Sam?' he asked, thinking their four-year-old had woken.

'It doesn't sound like him . . . I think it's coming from outside — from the verandah,' his wife replied.

Reverend Williams rose from his favourite chair and slipped out onto the vicarage's wide wooden verandah. He returned to the lounge a few moments later with a small bundle gently cradled in his arms. Wrapped inside was a tiny baby girl, probably only a few hours old, abandoned on the doorstep.

He teased his teenage sons, 'Which one of you had something to do with this!' But as he expected, the nameless child remained a mystery. She spent her first night nestled in an old cane clothes basket carefully positioned on the floor of Reverend and Mrs Williams's bedroom.

The next morning Reverend Williams told his local policeman of the unusual 'gift' and then arranged for the foundling to go to a state-run receiving home for children who had nowhere else to go. The arrangements were met with floods of tears from his seven-year-old daughter, who had been enraptured by the prospect of another sister in a family dominated by boys. Her father tried to explain that the family couldn't keep the mystery child because he already had eleven children of his own to provide for.

The baby, legally named after the area she was abandoned in, was cared for at the receiving home for the first two months of her life, fostered until she was about six months old, and then adopted and renamed. The final adoption order was granted when she was ten months old.

Sixty-five years later Helen Stanley began a seemingly impossible search for the woman who gave birth to her and then left her on a vicar's doorstep without a single clue to her origins. She had been happily married for more than forty years and was a grandmother after raising five sons of her own. But the questions about her origins had not faded with time; if anything, they had grown stronger.

Seated in a large soft lounge chair in her neat front lounge, the spring sunshine streaming in through modern ranchsliders recently added to the 1940s suburban home, Helen reflects back on her childhood.

'I was one of the lucky ones,' she says thoughtfully. 'In the circumstances of how I was left I have no doubt that if I hadn't been adopted I would have grown up in an orphanage and wouldn't have had a great deal of the opportunities in life which I have had. I was an only child and though times were hard — it was coming up to the Depression — I really had a very, very good life, which I owe entirely to my adoptive parents. I don't remember a great deal from when I was very young, but I do remember that they didn't want to know anything about the baby's origins. Their worst fear was that somebody would come and claim the baby once they'd got it.'

Perhaps it was that fear which prevented Helen's parents from telling her she was adopted, but, like many adoptees of her generation, it was a case of everyone in the neighbourhood except her knowing that she was not her parents' natural daughter — and the truth was bound to come out in less than perfect circumstances. Helen clearly remembers the revelation.

'I was about eleven or twelve when I found out. It was at primary school — I think perhaps I was rather a bossy child — and I was trying to organise some sport or other. I was telling this girl I couldn't stand to do something or go somewhere, when she just blew up.'

'Your mother's not your mother and your father's not your father, so shut up,' the little minx shouted at Helen, who now repeats the words in the same venomous tone in which they were originally uttered.

'I went home from school and asked my mother what she meant, and though my parents were very Victorian in their outlook, English and quite old to adopt a child, she never hesitated. She told me about my being left on the vicar's doorstep and that I was the baby they'd waited for, one that didn't have any contacts and nobody knew anything about. When I look back I'm quite amazed that she told me, because she could have denied it completely. But at the time I was absolutely shattered. I didn't know terribly much about adoption as such, and I didn't know anyone else in the same position. I was all at sea for quite a long time, and my parents, once having told me, didn't want to continue talking about it. It was hardly ever mentioned, but I do remember overhearing a conversation about it just after that. It was election time, we didn't have a car then, and a lady came to the house to take my parents up to vote. On the mantelpiece was a photograph of one of my father's sisters in England and this woman went over, picked it up, and turned to my mother and said, "Is this Helen's real mother?" I was quite like her but there was no connection at all.'

Helen was a bright and musically gifted child, and with her parents' encouragement she became a teacher. In her early twenties, and again with her parents' blessing, she married and had her own family. But the question mark 'Who am I?' hung over her for many years, though she doubts whether she would have seriously searched for her birth mother — if she had had the necessary information — in her adoptive parents' lifetimes. (They were both dead when she turned forty.)

'Over the years I'd approached people who I thought might know something — a vicar who had helped other adoptees and some of my parents' friends from where I grew up — but of course nobody did. Then I heard about the Adult Adoption Information Bill, though it was on and off for a long time. My husband — he's been very supportive — would talk about the fact that I might be able to find something out, but I was very casual about it because I just had a feeling the Bill might never be passed — then it was. My husband said, "Now you can get cracking," and then I got cold feet — I thought I might find out something I didn't want to know about, which of course I have done,' she says, hinting at the story she is about to tell, distressed yet fascinated by the truth of her birth.

Helen applied for her original birth certificate, but because of the unusual circumstances no clues to her birth parents' identities were revealed on the official record of birth. However, the change in law meant the Social Welfare Department was now willing to search its adoption files for information about an adoptee's origins.

'John Taylor from Social Welfare came out to see me with all the photocopies of different things about where I'd been and what had happened,' Helen says. 'I'll never forget that afternoon — I couldn't work out why he was coming to see me instead of just sending the pieces of paper, but it never dawned on me that there might be something a bit peculiar. He's a very nice chap but he was very ill at ease. He had a cup of tea and sat there with these folded papers.'

'What do you know about your origins?' John asked Helen.

'Well, all I really know is that I was left on a vicar's doorstep in Opawa and eventually adopted . . . that's about all really.'

'You could just about see the worry falling away from him!' Helen smiles. 'He thought he might have to tell me that and was worried about how I might react.'

John spent about an hour and a half explaining what few details his pieces of paper revealed. Amongst the papers were newspaper reports from 1922, describing the legal procedures surrounding the naming of the baby abandoned in Opawa. Helen was fascinated to hear that her original Christian names were Jane Helen, as requested by the matron of the receiving home, and her surname was bestowed by a judge, who was reported as saying: 'As a surname it shall be called after the locality in which it was found — Opawa. I do not want to give it a name that will cause stigma to anyone else and Opawa is a euphonious name.'

The newspaper reports described three-month-old Jane Helen Opawa as a 'bonny baby' who 'carried herself with considerable dignity', adding that she was not particularly interested in the name bestowal hearing!

Helen also heard for the first time that she had been fostered for several months before being adopted, and still wonders whether her adoptive parents ever knew that.

'I imagine you'll find it difficult to accept that after all this time that's all I can tell you,' John said. 'You can't really go any further now . . . I can't think of any other way to find out anything more.'

Apologetically repeating 'you can't go any further now', John packed away his papers, thanked Helen for the tea and made his way to the door. He then turned, unsure of the idea that had just formed in his mind, hesitant to put it into words.

'You know there is another way,' he said. 'I've got a good friend who's a journalist with the *Star* — Tony Smith — he's written quite a lot of articles about adoption and he's very interested in it. I'm sure he'd be interested in your case . . . How would you like him to come out and talk to you and print an article?'

'No way! I just couldn't,' Helen said quickly, shocked at the thought of exposing her personal life to public scrutiny.

'I think you should at least think about it, because he's had some great successes and I'm sure he'd be very helpful. I don't want to push it on you . . . but that's your last chance, that or nothing.'

'I'm not a public person,' Helen says, recalling the provocative 'that or nothing' John had left her with. 'I thought I can't do that — my children were quite anti the whole thing and I didn't want to do anything more that would upset them. One of my sons had said he thought it was a slur on my adoptive parents to be fiddling around trying to find out who my natural parents were, but I said to him, I got a bit cross really, "You know who your parents are . . . there are many things over the years that upset you when you don't know. Think about how many times I've been asked by doctors to fill out a form about the medical history of my parents. For years I used to put it in for my adoptive parents and thought that would do, but it was utter nonsense."

'Then a couple of months later, just out the blue, I decided to ring Tony Smith. I hadn't stopped to think that it could be anonymous, but Tony said my real name didn't have to go into it all. He wrote the article and really made a wonderful job of it but it came out on the font page!'

Helen's story began:

FINAL PLEA OVER PAST

By Tony Smith

A woman abandoned as a baby on a vicar's doorstep 65 years ago is making a last-ditch attempt to fit together the missing pieces of her genetic jigsaw.

The woman, who declined to be named, recently applied under the new Adult Adoption Information Act for a copy of her birth certificate.

She received the certificate but because she was abandoned as an infant it did not contain details of her birth parents' identities.

'It was frustrating,' she said.

'I realise because it happened 65 years ago my birth mother is almost surely dead.

'But I just hope she might have told someone about it over the years and that any publicity might lead to me contacting any of my relatives.'

—*Star*, January 1987

The story was printed on a Wednesday, and the next afternoon, about two o'clock, Helen's telephone rang.

'Mrs Stanley? Tony Smith from the *Star* here . . . I think I've got some good news . . . A lady's just rung me about yesterday's story. She want to remain anonymous but she'd like you to ring her — it's a toll call — she thinks she might have some information for you . . .'

The excitement and dread of the unknown are still evident in Helen's voice. 'I kept sitting there by the phone, thinking I'll ring, no I'll do it later, no now. I didn't know what to think about ringing — it was all so exciting but it was so new on top of the article, it was so quick. But I got up my courage and rang her . . .'

'Hello, Nancy? . . . Tony Smith from the *Star* has given me your number — he said you rang him about yesterday's article,' Helen said hesitantly to the woman who answered the phone. 'He said you might have some information for me?'

'Yes, well I think so. I read the article and I don't think there would be two circumstances the same, not at the same time and in the same place. And I kept thinking that if I held the key, then surely you've got a right to know,' the woman of about Helen's age began. 'If I'm right, your mother's name was Mrs Heron, Maude Heron . . . she and my mother were very great friends many years ago when they lived not far from each other . . . My mother told me — it must be about twenty years ago — how Mrs Heron had a child in 1921 and had to give it away, left her on the vicar's doorstep in Opawa . . . please don't be too harsh on your mother, because she really was absolutely desperate when you were born, absolutely desperate.'

In the forty-five-minute conversation Helen prompted Nancy for every detail she could possibly remember about Maude Heron, her mother, who had passed away thirty years earlier. But while Helen's memory of the conversation, five months later, is crystal-clear, the full background to her birth and the story of her mother's life is painful to repeat, impossible to tell confidently, directly, and without withdrawing into the silence of her own thoughts. Ten months later she is able to say the words that sum up Nancy's information, letters from two of Reverend Williams' children (he is no longer alive), and her own painstaking searches of birth, marriage and death certificates.

'My mother had five daughters, four of whom were illegitimate. The first one was fostered and then when my mother married was taken into the family. The second one was adopted from birth by the grandparents, Maude's parents. I'm the third. The fourth was the child of her husband, before they were married. The fifth was their legitimate daughter.'

Maude was born in the mid 1890s and grew up in a small New Zealand town, the second eldest daughter in a large family dominated by girls. She was a tall, solidly built but attractive young woman of twenty when her first daughter, who was put into the care of foster parents, was born. Strangely, the pregnancy — like her others — was never obvious and when the second child arrived, eighteen months later, it appears that Maude's parents decided the best course for all was for them to adopt the child from birth and care for her as they would another child of their own — and for Maude to leave the family home. She found employment as a nanny in a large stately home on the outskirts of the nearest city. Helen was born a year and a half later and bears a striking resemblance to Maude's employer, a man still remembered in local history books and who would have been in his forties at the time. Shortly after Helen's birth, Maude took a job as housekeeper for a widower whose wife had died very suddenly, leaving him with two daughters of about five and seven. About a year later her fourth daughter was born. This time she married the father, her employer. The couple retrieved Maude's first daughter from foster care and, about eighteen months later, had another daughter. Maude is remembered by those who knew her as a 'wonderfully helpful person who was lots of fun, very musical and a wonderful mother'.

Helen is not bitter when speaking of her birth mother, but she cannot help but sadly wonder about why a woman would abandon her newly born child.

'I always felt that it was one of two things — either she had a very big family and just couldn't cope with things, and I know that happened sometimes, or she was an unmarried mother and had no means of supporting the child, which I understood when I had children of my own and didn't feel bitter about it,' she says sincerely. 'I had these two pictures in my mind and it turned out I was right. Nancy pleaded with me not to be too harsh on Maude, which I don't think I had been, but what I can't understand is why I was left when the previous two had been catered for. Also, for some reason I always felt I was the first one, I don't know why, but particularly when I found out there were others I thought I was probably the only illegitimate one. My own theory, for what it's worth, is that she was pregnant, and although you evidently could never tell because she was a biggish woman, it would have been hushed up by the owner of the property. Whether he was the one, or someone else — maybe a son — I feel he would have overridden anything she wanted to do, perhaps in order to save his position. Where could she have gone in those days? Where? There was nowhere, and I don't think she could have gone home again — she probably never told her parents — so she probably had to accept whatever he came up with. He might have even been the one who did the taking — it's not far from that house to the vicarage.'

Helen picks up several photocopied pages of print — an article about the man she suspects was her father, and whose family name is still well known in the district. A photograph is included with the words, the image adding considerable weight to her theory.

'I know he married several times and lived to a ripe old age. He bought the property (where Maude worked) and completely redesigned it and also the beautiful gardens which are still there. He was a prominent person in the area, a bit of a lad,' she laughs ironically, 'and from what the article said I think he would have been a very aggressive, arrogant sort of a man.' But while it all seems to fit, and Helen thinks about tracing her family tree, she will never be a hundred per cent certain of the identity of her birth father.

'But the story doesn't end there . . . the afternoon I first rang Nancy and she gave me the name of my mother, my husband, Bob, was there listening.'

'Well?' Bob asked when Helen put down the receiver and was looking through the notes she had scribbled down.

'The name, the surname, doesn't mean anything to me but I'm sure you know it — Heron,' she replied.

'Oh heavens, yes. We used to play with the Heron girls years ago . . . and there's Jill who married Peter Green — do you remember I went to his funeral, what was it, ten or fifteen years ago? Do you think they're related?'

'It seems so . . . Nancy said she thought I had three sisters — or rather half-sisters — May and Emily . . . and Jill. She said she thought Jill would be the best one to try and contact.'

'It was just so unbelievable,' Helen says. 'And it was quite shattering too because I felt that's where I should have been playing, I should have been in that situation with them. I rang Bob's sister and, probably because it was a family of girls, she remembered more than he could. But the amazing thing was that they could tell me all about the husband, what he looked like, what sort of person he was, and all about the girls — my half-sisters — but neither of them had any recollection of the mother whatsoever. All I can think is that she would have been in the background, making the tea, and just had a very low profile.

'It was all so strange — and there was another coincidence. During the war Bob was good friends with Peter, before he married Jill, but they didn't really see each other after the war till about twenty years ago, when Bob started going to the dawn services and they met up again. Peter asked if our boys would like to go fishing with him down near the estuary, so one day we all went down there. The boys and men went off fishing, and I was left at home to talk to the wife — who was Jill. We were never close friends, I don't think we're very much alike, but we used to see the family perhaps once or twice a year after that up until the husband died. I feel badly about not visiting her after that — you know how time slips by — but then we saw her at an RSA Christmas party a couple of years ago and caught up on what had happened over the years.'

Helen didn't rush to contact her sister, nervous at what the reaction might be. Instead she concentrated on working out exactly where each of the sisters fitted into the family. Birth, death and marriage records revealed the true picture — four sisters instead of Nancy's count of three, and the fact that Jill was the second eldest and the only illegitimate daughter who had spent all her childhood with her natural mother.

'When I first discovered Jill was my half-sister I wondered whether it would be easier to tell her, though we weren't close friends, or somebody I didn't know at all. I kept putting it off and then finally asked John Taylor from Social Welfare.'

'There's only one way you can approach this, and believe me I know,' John told Helen. 'You ring her up and say, "I haven't seen you in a long time and I'd like to come and see you and have a chat — it's a personal matter." '

'Oh no, I can't say that,' Helen replied. 'She'll think, "What the hell's going on!" I can't say that.'

'Yes, but you must say something like that because you're not just going to see her for a casual cup of tea,' John insisted. 'You've got to give her the opportunity to perhaps think back, not just land up there and spill all this out. You've got to be very careful how you do it — don't just start off about being left on a doorstep, in fact you don't really have to bring that into it at all. Just talk about it quite casually and say, "I wonder if you can help me," that sort of thing.'

'In the end I did exactly what he told me. I rang her one evening and she said, "Come in the morning, about ten o'clock." When I got off the phone I said to Bob, "I've really done it now, I don't know how I'm going to cope with it." I was in such a panic. I knew Jill was a great talker, but she's also very matter-of-fact and says exactly what she thinks without beating around the bush — she could say, "Right, there's the gate, I don't want to know about it," and that would be it, or she could say she didn't believe a word of it, or she could accept it, which I didn't think she would.

'Bob knew I'd either be quite elated or down to zero and he was adamant that he was going with me. I wanted to talk to Jill alone but I didn't know whether I'd be five minutes, ten minutes or hours, so I dropped Bob off near the house where he could go for a walk and we made a place where we'd meet every half-hour. At quarter past twelve, two and a quarter hours later, Jill was still telling me all about her family, all about her sisters, all about her son's wedding — I was pigeon-holing all the information and the more I heard the more I knew I couldn't be wrong in what I'd worked out — but I was also starting to panic and imagine Bob would be thinking she'd killed me! And I still hadn't told her why I was there.'

'I live on my own now,' Jill said, concluding the news of what had happened since the two women last saw each other, 'and I read the papers cover to cover these days.'

Helen summoned her courage and took the opening: 'Do you

remember an article in the *Star* a couple of months ago about somebody trying to find her family?'

'I've got a vague idea — I think I read it but I don't remember any of the details . . . that's what you've come about, isn't it? It's you, is it?'

'Yes, it's me.'

'I never thought of you being adopted . . . you've done some research into it?'

'Yes, quite a lot actually,' Helen said, still too nervous to put her thoughts into words.

'It's led to me, has it?'

'It would appear so . . . I've come because I thought perhaps you could help me — perhaps you may be able to see if I'm on the right track.' Helen paused, lost for words — how could she possibly say that Jill's mother was also her mother?

'Well come on, out with it . . . you should know me well enough to know that I can accept most things . . . what's the connection?' Jill prompted.

'What I've got to say is very difficult . . . I can't tell you, Jill.'

'You've come this far so you'll have to now . . . I know — it's Maude, isn't it?' Jill questioned, calling her mother by her Christian name.

'Yes.'

Jill jumped off her chair and rushed to find her birthday book, working out the ages of her sisters and where Helen fitted in. Realising she was talking with a sister she had never met and never known even existed, Jill stood staring for a moment before warmly hugging her new-found sibling.

'I always thought there must have been another one somewhere — fancy it being you!'

'Jill was absolutely marvellous,' Helen says, still elated by Jill's reaction. 'We're not very much alike in looks or as people but she has no doubts at all. The only part of the story she can't accept, although she knows it must be right, is why our mother catered for the other illegitimate children and not me.'

Helen has asked Nancy, the woman whose response to the newspaper was so valuable, if her mother remembers anything more about Maude and the child she abandoned. But Nancy's mother is now frail and losing her memory — all she can say to the question is: 'Baby? I forget, I forget.' And the only thing Nancy has been able to add to her original information is that Helen looks very much like Maude. 'I can't see it really,' Helen says, 'though I'm very much like the only legitimate daughter, which is quite amazing.

'I also heard from a lady who knew my foster family very well,' she adds. 'She said they used to talk about me and how much my foster mother would have liked to keep me but wouldn't because she was already a widow with three children — I'd wondered why my foster family hadn't adopted me.'

Helen would love to meet her other sisters but Jill is against the idea, saying May, Emily and Bev would not accept her, though she has introduced Helen to May, the eldest sister, as just a friend. While Helen and Jill have formed a strong friendship, the other sisters are not close and rarely see one another.

'Emily, who was adopted by her grandparents, apparently doesn't even admit that Maude was her mother — or doesn't want to know,' Helen explains. 'And May evidently has a real chip on her shoulder because she was shifted around from one foster home to another until her mother could take her. Jill was the one who was closest to her mother, obviously because she was with her mother all the time, and for her years is very broad in her outlook — as I am now, but I wouldn't have been then because I had such a narrow upbringing. Jill can accept Maude for what she was, and she says she was a marvellous mother and was very kind.

'John [from Social Welfare] feels I have no right to choose who I contact and who I don't. He says they all have a right to know, but because I'm very concerned about the whole story, particularly where I fit in, it's pretty tough to know what to do.'

Outsiders might say Helen would have been saved a great deal of pain and trauma if she had not sought the truth about her birth, and she readily admits she was deeply disturbed by the story of her origins. But she is also firm in her response to any suggestion that she would have been better off not knowing. 'I'm glad I found out . . . no matter how terrible the truth had been it would still have been beneficial.'

Apart from the need to know about the circumstances of birth, Helen also sees the question mark over family medical history as an important aspect of adoption. 'In the past I'd give my adoptive parents' medical background,' she says, 'but I don't worry any more about saying I was adopted and now know that my mother died of breast cancer — there was a little chill for a second when I found that out, but I'm now older than she was and my problems aren't in that area at all.'

Helen speaks softly when she thinks about her birth mother's death. 'I'd hoped Maude might still be alive,' she says. 'I realised I was in my sixties, and there was only a very slim chance, but I had in my mind that she could have been a teenager when I was born and might still be alive . . . I felt very sad,' she says simply, unable to find the words to express her grief for the woman she will never meet and will probably never fully understand.

'It's only a week or two ago that I said to Bob, "A lot of these people, like my mother and my foster mother, they've all died, they're not here anymore — why didn't I do this years ago?" He just looked at me and reminded me that it was only recently that the law was changed . . . so it's not too late, almost, but not quite.

'And now that I know I think I've got a different attitude towards things. I always felt worthless, I know it sounds silly, but I felt as though I didn't belong anywhere — there was just that missing link. My husband reckons it's made a big difference to me as a person, that I've got more confidence in myself now, even in my judgments.

'I guess I'm more at peace now . . . all those years it was just a question mark: "Who am I?" '

FOUR

Rounding things out a bit: Julie

Julie was adopted as a baby in 1959. Twenty-seven years later she applied for a copy of her original birth certificate through the Adult Adoption Information Act. With the bare details the certificate provided she searched birth, death and marriage records and electoral rolls eventually to discover her birth mother had left New Zealand and settled in Australia. Julie successfully made contact and the two women have since become good friends through regular letters across the Tasman. They hope to meet sometime in the future but are in no great rush to take that step for fear of hurting the precious but delicate relationship they are building.

Julie is a confident and likeable woman, the sort of person it's easy to warm to and enjoyable to talk with over morning tea. She speaks with affection of her husband, Stephen, a surveyor, and is relaxed with their two small children who play happily around her, only occasionally demanding her sole attention while she tells of her experiences of adoption.

Julie grew up knowing she was adopted and first thought about attempting to trace her birth mother when she was a teenager in the 1970s, but the thought remained just that, something in the back of her mind, never urgent enough to push her into a battle against the secrecy surrounding her birth. She attributes her lack of action to her secure childhood and full life as a young adult, combined with the legal barriers surrounding information about her birth origins. Then the Adult Adoption Information Bill became law and many of those barriers dissolved.

'I wasn't actually all that curious,' she says. 'What really pushed

me into searching was that the legislation made it easy, the
barriers had gone, the opportunity was there and the more I
thought about it the more I wanted to take it. If there hadn't
been a change in law I might just still be wondering about it
every now and then — and possibly have done something when
I was older and had more time.

'I grew up with my adoption being a perfectly normal thing. I
always knew about it, the family all knew, it wasn't a big secret
or a traumatic piece of information that was dropped on me as
a teenager — which happened to a friend I went to school with.
She was told she was adopted when she was thirteen and went
quite off the wall for a while. It changed her personality drastically
and she's never really got to the point where she's forgiven her
parents. But I can't even remember being told, though I do
remember my parents had this neat book about an adopted
child. It was a storybook with pictures, quite old-fashioned, but
I was really fond of it and it was probably a bed-time story for
quite some time. I think that's how they introduced it, making
adoption a normal subject. I can also remember the feeling that
I was special and Greg, my brother who's not adopted, was special, but we were special for different reasons and there was no
favouritism and no big deal.

'I felt very secure in that family, but I think as a teenager I had
more problems knowing who I was than if I hadn't been adopted.
There were a few rough years with Mum and Dad — I wasn't the
easiest teenager in the world and my brother was the one who'd
do everything right, but then he's a different personality, less
inclined to rock the boat than I am. And the fact that I was
adopted was a good lever to use because it was the one thing that
made me a bit different, and I used it to the hilt because it suited
me when I was being obnoxious!' Julie laughs with some embarrassment now. 'I'd say things like: "If I find my birth parents
they'll let me do this . . . I hate you because you won't." I was
pretty good at that sort of thing as a teenager and could run rings
around my parents completely but they dealt with it very well
and I didn't get away with a great deal — though I must have
been pretty hard to live with. But it never became a great
problem and I don't think I'm any the worse for it, though I

s'pose they came out of it feeling a bit bedraggled!

'When I was about seventeen Mum and Dad told me all they knew about my background but it wasn't very much. They knew I came from a Protestant family, that the medical history was pretty well clear, that my birth mother was young and solo and that I'd been given the name Leigh. But I think if I'd searched then, or when I was between about eighteen and twenty-one and was far further away from my family than I am now, perhaps I would have gone overboard and stomped on Mum and Dad's feelings by not including them. The thought of searching cropped up again with more intensity when the boys were born, because you always wonder where they get things from. There was also very much the feeling, quite apart from the family, that everything stopped with me — and it's amazing just what does show up in children. So when the law was passed, just after Jonathan was born, I started to become more curious — just because the information was more easily accessible.

'I spent a lot of time considering the implications. I considered putting a veto on my information as a precaution, a form of protection, but it seemed unfair — if I was going to search and lay myself open to being hurt or being rejected it was silly to place a veto,' she says.

Julie applied for a copy of her original birth certificate. No veto had been placed by her birth mother, the only parent named, and as required under the law she received the certificate through an approved counsellor. Her original name was Leanne (rather than the Leigh remembered by her adoptive parents) Parks. Her birth mother's name was Diana Parks, aged nineteen at the time of birth. Her address was given simply as Wellington. Julie had grown up in Blenheim, where her adoptive parents still live, and settled in Christchurch as an adult.

'When I saw the counsellor I was only interested in getting my birth certificate and just finding out the name,' she says. 'I was quite philosophical about it all. I talked to her and thought it was all clear and sorted out. I'd discussed it with Stephen, my husband, with Mum and Dad and friends and cousins. But I still wonder whether I was protecting myself against there being nothing on the birth certificate for me to go on, because I'd read about

people who had been devastated by vetoes; perhaps it was a case
of subconsciously having every intention of going ahead with a
search right from the start but telling myself I wasn't all that
interested, the way you sometimes protect yourself. But it just
escalates — you can't just find out one little bit of information
without wanting to know the rest — and once I had the name
it started to become quite important, though I hadn't set out
with any intention of it being so. It became more than just
curiosity, it was, "If I don't find out I'm going to imagine all sorts
of things and always wonder." Before, it had just been, "I wonder
what she's like." I could take it or leave it. I couldn't now because
it was necessary to know more.

'I discussed it all with Mum and Dad, saying that if they dis-
agreed it wouldn't changed my decision to search, but I wanted
to know what they thought. They were quite happy. Mum could
understand, but then women tend to have the same kind of
feelings, though Dad was a little bit threatened at first, I think
over his position in my life. He didn't actually say that, but it was
the sort of feeling I got. That's all reconciled now — probably
because they were part of it, they were included in what I was
doing.'

But knowing the name, age and location of someone nearly
thirty years ago does not mean they will automatically appear in
the current electoral roll and telephone book, and Julie's birth
mother Diana was not easy to locate. An already planned family
holiday, which included several days with friends in Wellington,
provided the perfect opportunity for Julie to learn the value of
official birth, death and marriage records held at Levin House,
in Lower Hutt, twenty minutes' drive from where the family was
staying.

'I got Diana's birth certificate,' she says, remembering the long
but exciting hours of work involved. 'There wasn't a marriage
certificate, but I got her parents' marriage certificate, which gave
me a few other family members' names, and then her father's
death certificate — he'd dropped off the electoral roll so I
assumed he died and that there would be a death notice. I
searched the papers in the General Assembly Library and I
found it — they usually just put "loving daughter Diana" or

something like that — but I was in luck, it actually had her married name, Stone, and place of residence, Melbourne, Australia. I had to be a bit devious about getting her current address — I rang an uncle and pretended to be an old friend of my birth mother who had lost touch!' Julie laughs, though still a little uncomfortable with the memory of her amateur detective work.

'One of the things that amazed me when I started searching was how much information you could find out about family history just from the records. I knew where the family had lived, what jobs her father had and that her parents had split up and divorced — quite intimate family details that in some ways you almost feel you don't have a right to, or that it's an imposition on the family. And of course you tend to make assumptions. I come from a very stable family, we always lived in the same place, but Diana's family had moved around quite a lot. It sounds snobby and I don't mean it to, but you do get impressions about a family that has moved a lot, and you do tend to draw conclusions about their lifestyle — which might be completely wrong. But then perhaps it's another way of protecting yourself, thinking that if it's someone you haven't got a hope of having anything in common with and just don't like, then you can't be hurt.'

But having come this far, the next question was how to make contact with a woman in Australia whose family might have no knowledge of a long-buried secret, and who might not be aware of the change in New Zealand law that had allowed Julie access to the identifying information.

'I wondered whether I should go through Social Welfare and have the Australian equivalent contact her,' she says. 'A friend suggested it might be a good idea to ask a friend we knew in Melbourne to contact her, but I didn't think it was fair to put her in that position, though I did ask her to look at the house — she said it was just a nice family home but there was no one around when she drove past. Other friends pushed the point that I might be laying myself open to be hurt and mightn't be able to cope. Someone suggested I should go through a lawyer but that seemed too formal. Stephen also thought I was really laying myself open to be badly hurt, but then he realised how important it was and that I'd put a lot of thought into it. In the end it boiled

down to taking the risk and sending a letter, though I thought
perhaps I shouldn't send it to her home in case she had a husband who opened all her mail and if he didn't know about it —
well, some women live in appalling conditions. My parents were
of the opinion that I should just write, and it was important to
me that I wrote. Perhaps it was an unfair gamble on my part; the
risk was definitely there and I did agonise over it for some time,
but if that was the only way I could get round it I had to do it.
I decided I had some rights too because my needs were also quite
important.'

Julie wrote, and rewrote, the letter to her birth mother, tearing
up each version until she was happy the words expressed her
desire for a reply but were low-key, open and considerate of
Diana's feelings and current life. She hoped the mention of
grandchildren might be a motivating factor, but at the same time
she was wary of saying too much in fear of rejection or, at the
other end of the scale, a gushy reply that Diana would be on the
first flight across the Tasman. In the back of her mind was also
the possibility that she might have made some disastrous error
in her search and have the wrong woman. Presuming she had the
right woman, 'Dear Mrs Stone' was too formal, and she chose to
write:

Dear Diana,
My name is Julie Debra Harris, née Edmonton, but I was born
Leanne Parks on 29 April 1959.
    I have managed to trace you because the law in New Zealand
recently changed and through the new Adult Adoption Information Act I was able to obtain a copy of my original birth certificate. I then traced you through the electoral rolls, using your
father's name. I realise it might seem like an invasion of privacy
and that my letter will probably raise mixed feelings for you but
having got this far I feel I must write.
    I grew up in Blenheim and have a brother who is three years
older than me and is my adoptive parents' natural son. I trained
as a primary school teacher and now work part time near where
we live in Christchurch. I am married and we have two sons,
Jonathan, who is two, and Timothy, who turned five last week.
    This letter will probably come as a big shock for you, particu-
larly because you may not be aware of the recent change in law,

but I would really appreciate some sort of reply. If I don't hear from you I won't try to contact you again.

Julie

Overestimating the time letters take to cross the Tasman, Julie had not even started to watch out for the postie each morning when a letter arrived from Melbourne just seven days later.

Dear Julie,
Thank you for your letter — I'm glad you decided to write to me. I've thought about you often, and now it seems so strange to be actually writing to you after all this time . . .

With love

Diana

'I couldn't have expected a nicer letter back. It was a short letter but she was open and pleased about the contact and accepted me without question,' Julie says, aware of Diana's reticence over allowing other eyes to see her private letters. 'I was more excited than I thought I'd be. I rang Stephen at work and raced up to see a friend who knew all about it. It's hard now to think of not having got the response I did, because it was so nice.'

Julie and Diana began writing regularly to each other, their letters becoming more chatty and relaxed as the months passed, the delicate relationship growing into friendship. Distance is a barrier to meeting, but while both women could find the money for airfares, neither feels an urgency to meet face to face, knowing that will come in time. They have exchanged photographs and written about their lives and families, though Diana has only briefly mentioned the circumstances of her daughter's adoption. As Julie had imagined, her mother was single when she learnt she was pregnant, decided to adopt because of the extreme pressures on an unmarried woman with a child in the 1950s, and later married and had other children.

'It's not an issue with me,' she says. ' At that time adoption was what you did; you didn't have the social support, there was far more stigma attached and you were extremely brave if you did keep a child. She's said nothing about the birth except that it was easy. She only got a glimpse of me and wanted to see more of me, wanted to hold me, but typical of the times she was told it was better not to see me, to go away and forget, and they seemed to have absolutely no conception that you just don't forget. I think it was very similar to the way most women were treated and expected to deal with it — "You've made a mistake, go away and forget, start again, get married and have a baby as soon as possible." Diana says she didn't forget, but her way of reconciling it to herself was that she'd created a family for somebody else, made other people happy, and she's pleased now to realise that's true.

'She went to Australia not long after I was born, ostensibly on a working holiday, and then met her husband and stayed there. From what I can gather, he's always been extremely understanding, but I did get the impression he felt really threatened by me on behalf of their children. In one of her first letters there was a sentence about showing my letter to her husband and he had said he wouldn't stop her from writing. That made me prickle because I loathe the thought of a spouse preventing their partner from doing something. But then he had no idea what I was like. It's quite understandable that he could have thought, "God, the kids don't know about her," (which they didn't), "What are we going to do, what is she going to do to this family?" So in the next letter I spent time trying to reassure him that I wasn't about to upset anyone more than I already had, that wasn't my reason for writing.

'She also said she'd actually named me Katrina but had no say in anything once she'd decided to give me up for adoption, and the staff at the home I was born in named me Leanne, though she didn't have a clue about that till I wrote. My brother mentioned that it's quite strange to realise somebody has always thought of me as Katrina, and you do project a certain personality on people from their name. It's like when you read a book and imagine all the characters, then when you see the movie and they're portrayed in a completely different way you have to do quite a bit of adjustment in your mind. Diana doesn't seem to have had any difficulty with the transition — but then she definitely hadn't forgotten me. She said one of her daughter's birthday was just several days after mine and that was always a difficult time of year; she would fall apart a bit around my birthday and then pull herself together about a week later.

'I asked about my father, not so much because I felt any real need to contact him in the same way as I did her, but more to complete the history, to tie up the loose ends. We'd been writing for about six months and she hadn't mentioned anything, then when I asked she said she'd rather tell me in person than in a letter because she still hadn't told anybody who he was, and that's fine by me. I still don't know what the circumstances were. I gather it was fairly horrific, but whether it was her family's reaction, I don't know. She said people drew all sorts of conclusions at the time and she allowed them to do that, and I think there was a big rift between her and her mother, which has only healed a bit in the last few years. It will be quite interesting to hear what she has to say about my father, but I've no idea whether I want to meet him — it's quite a different thing approaching a man, rather than a woman, and saying, "Oi! Remember 1959!" Maybe he'd be pleased, or maybe she never told him about me.

'But having contact with Diana has explained a lot to me. There were always things I wondered about, like where do I get certain things from? What makes me like I am? A lot of it must be environment — we were brought up in a family where you were encouraged to read, find things out for yourself and try to do what you chose to do — but there were lots of things quite separate from circumstance and environment that I wondered about. I was always far more argumentative than anyone in the family, while my brother was far more like Mum and Dad in personality than I was, though perhaps that comes from my birth father, rather than Diana. But with every letter from her I think, that's just like me, there's something in there that's just like me. We look quite a lot alike, but apart from that there are various traits we have in common, particularly animal instincts. I can remember Mum saying, "You must come from farming stock because you surely don't get that from us," and she was right! Diana grew up on a farm and also worked outside with the family. We lived in a rural town, and perhaps it was that influence, but it was quite alien for Mum and Dad to have anyone wanting a horse or coming home smelling of sheep sheds and just loving it! They didn't discourage me, but then they didn't encourage me; it was more, "You look after that horse and don't bring it home where it can piddle on the grass!" The other thing that stands out is that Diana reads a lot, and I couldn't survive without reading, though I grew up in a family where books are the norm. There are lots of other things you could tie in if you wanted to, but they're just as likely to be from the upbringing I had, and because Diana's from a middle-class European-type family, the type of family I grew up with, you expect there to be some similarities in the kind of person you become — but I think there is more to it than that.'

Julie and Diana are beginning to look ahead towards the day they meet, but there is no rush. Julie is confident it will happen when the time is right.

'I actually said in one letter I was quite pleased we lived so far away because I didn't want to rush things, I was looking forward to meeting her, but it was important that we had a good base,' Julie says. 'I thought perhaps I might be hurting her saying that, but I've got the impression that's not so. There's also the problem that her children don't know anything about me and I'd feel wrong about going over there to find I wasn't free to go to her house, though I suppose it doesn't matter if she comes over here. I haven't pushed this issue and in her latest letter she said she was thinking about telling them.

'I was also pleased when she referred to herself in one letter as the boys' grandmother — that's what she is and I was pleased that it came from her, that she feels comfortable with it. But she's not "Mum" and I don't think she ever will be, it's not necessary. It's hard to explain — she's my birth mother but she's not actually the one who has been around when things have gone well or badly — making contact and building a relationship are far more important than thinking of her as "Mother". Mum is "Mum", and quite apart from everything else, I think she'd be hurt, where nothing else has hurt her, because that's her name. I'd no more call Diana "Mum" than fly to the moon; there are other aspects that are important, being friends and just having things in common no one else has.

'Knowing Diana, I don't think it's changed me but it's given me another dimension, rounded things out a little bit. I feel very normal in all of this, I've been conscious of not needing to find another family, and writing and remembering things I haven't thought about in years has made me realise how loved I was by my adoptive parents and what a good childhood I had. They're my parents in all but biology really, and I wouldn't change them for the world.'

FIVE

I couldn't be Maori or Pakeha: Patricia

Born in 1950, Patricia was fourteen when she found out she was adopted, and that her 'aunt' was in fact her birth mother. She had always wondered whether she was different in some way from her family because her brothers and sisters looked like a mixture of her Maori mum and Pakeha dad, but she only looked like her mum.

Patricia is also a birth mother.

Patricia sits on a well-worn 1960s-style couch, which faces a large colour television set in the far corner of her lounge. She's obviously nervous at the prospect of being interviewed, and finds herself a solid cut-glass ashtray before lighting a cigarette. She apologises if her home seems untidy, but while the lounge could possibly do with a fresh coat of paint, it is clean and tidy, as is the rest of the house. She relaxes as the time passes and her 'story' unfolds. 'I was fourteen before I found out I was adopted,' she says. 'The word adopted was never mentioned before that, nothing was said. I was with an aunt of mine one day, who is actually my real mother plus my adopted mother's sister, and she said to a neighbour, "Patricia is adopted." I thought, jeez, that's strange, so I went home to my mum and said, "Am I adopted?" Well, she was really shocked.

'"Who told you that? I want to know who said this," she said.

'"I heard it from my aunt."

'"Ooh!"

'I was kind of rushed out of the room and she rang up my aunt and was really irate about the whole thing. Then my dad came home and I mentioned it again.

'He said, "What's going on? What's happened?"'

'My mum said, "That big mouth told Patricia what's happened, what's gone on."'

'They thought I knew my aunt was my real mum, but I didn't, I'd just heard her say I was adopted. But that night my dad said, "I think it's about time we told Patricia who she really is." So she did . . . from what I understand, the circumstances of why they adopted me were that my real mother, my adopted mum's older sister, had too many children. She had three children in one year. And that's when I also learnt I was a twin — and that my twin sister had died. I was quite amazed by all this coming out at once, and it was all pretty traumatic. My real mother decided to give me to my grandmother, and because her younger sister [Patricia's aunt and later adoptive mother] was at home all the time, she kind of looked after me like I was her child. She was only about seventeen then, and when she got married she'd got so attached to me she said she wanted to keep me. Mum and Dad told it to me by saying all sorts of nice things, that I was really special, and how much my mum loved me and couldn't go without me, and I accepted that. But there was also lots of crying that night, and saying all these different things, and I didn't really know what to do.

'Although I didn't know before that, earlier on in my life I knew something was drastically wrong because my dad, my adopted dad, is white, and my mother is a Maori, and I used to think I was different from my brothers and sisters, but then I thought maybe I just looked like my mum, and I seemed to look very much like her. I can also remember going to school and they said, "All the Maori children stand up," and I never did. This was when I was only about five. And they said, "Come on, Patricia, get up," and of course I said, "No, because my dad is a Pakeha." I was a bit lost, and of course I started to recall all those things when I found out I was adopted and I thought, gee, I always thought something was different. I really loved my dad and had always thought he was my real dad and that I just looked the same as my mum.

'There's a lot of informal adoption in my immediate family, but I was a secret. No one really says too much in my family about how these things happen, but I believe that they didn't like my real father, that is, my grandfather didn't. He was a Maori elder and had quite a lot of say over what was going to happen. The younger people kind of respected what the elders said, and as he didn't like my real father, he said that my real mother and father should never come back and claim me from my grandmother or my mum — I gather it was kind of like a death wish, his last words before his death. I was only three months old then — that's the whole thing of why it was all kept quiet . . . in those times it actually stood really firm, not like today, where you could say, "Well I don't really agree, I don't think I could hold to such a promise."

'And I don't know why, but I'd always heard that my real mother wasn't a very nice lady, even though I didn't know she was my mother. But I basically thought she was quite a nice person, somehow to me she seemed okay. It all comes back to me now as I start putting things together — I grew up knowing her as my aunty, but I remember she actually said to me one day, "I'm really your mother," and I just looked at her and thought maybe she was just saying something that was totally wrong — but I'm just amazed why I never ever questioned what she was saying. I think I knew that if I said that little bit too much I was going to get into trouble, for some unknown reason. If I asked too many questions I was going to get into something that really wasn't for my ears, funnily enough. I sensed there was something not quite right.

'Also I've recently found out I was never legally adopted. I'd never looked at my birth certificate, it just didn't worry me. You see, my [adoptive] mother had ways of covering it up — she would go in and do my applications and different things like that, fill everything in for me. She was a woman who always did things for us all the time, so I was none the wiser to what was going on, but it must have been really hard for her, running around doing things to cover up. To me it's like a double life. Oh God! It's a real mix-up and I thought, jeez, I don't belong anywhere. It's given me a real terrible complex about where I actually belong, and sometimes I just want to swear and curse because I don't know what I'm doing, or who I am, or where I should be.

'I didn't think much about it till I was sixteen and went through a kind of a crisis where I needed to know exactly where I was, because I thought to myself, Jesus, all my cousins are really my real brothers and sisters. I was a bit scared of my real mother then, because of what my mum said about her being really quite bad. I was afraid of seeing her, but I did, and it was at my own doing because I wanted to know her. Her husband is my real father, and I asked her all about him because he's a really interesting person. He actually comes from South America and is really artistic — I sometimes look at him and think, no wonder I'm really interested in the arts. When I was growing up I wanted to be an artist, and my mother always deterred me from being one. They wanted me to be an office girl or something like that, and sent me to all the best schools. I did work in an office but I didn't really like it. I just did whatever work there was, because I really wanted to travel and I did. I went to Australia and some Asian countries. I haven't been to Europe or anything but I wanted to.'

Patricia returned to New Zealand, and then married when she was twenty-two. Four years later the couple separated, and she went back to work to support her two children. It was the Christmas season, the time of year for work parties and large amounts of alcohol.

'I got pregnant just after I separated and went back to work,' she says, lighting another cigarette. 'Right up to today I detest Christmas parties, because that's what it was all about. He was married and I knew nothing would come out of it because we were just work friends, that was all, and I didn't tell him. I already had a daughter and a son,' she explains, beginning to withdraw into her own thoughts. 'I had her . . . I'd debated whether I should have an abortion or adoption . . . when she was born I thought I couldn't give her up and decided to keep her. I did, but I know now that I had post-natal depression, and I was doing lots of things that were really wrong. It was all pretty hard for me to cope with, so when Suzie was three months old I adopted her out. I thought I'd give her up for a better life, kind of like what my mother did for me — she said she gave me up so as I could have a better life.

I just didn't understand the whole system, I didn't know how I was going to cope with my finances and everything, I didn't know about the Domestic Purposes Benefit — if I'd known a bit more about that I would have kept her. And there was the fact that my family didn't want her either because it was out of marriage. Right up to today they won't acknowledge that I had Suzie, and I think a lot of it is that I grew up in a life where they wanted everything right for me, their "special" girl. I mean they paid lots of money giving me everything — that's what they say — and even now I feel like I'm under some sort of obligation to them because of all this money they paid out for me. But I think, aren't all parents meant to give their kids a good education and everything? They made me feel I was obligated. And I come from a strict religious family, so of course they expect you to marry and be faithful to your husband and all this. The fact that I separated and had a child . . . it was like I was doomed.

'I breast-fed Suzie till the morning she was adopted . . . I don't ever want to have to live through an experience like that again. Oh jeez, I've had some experiences but that was the worst . . . having to sign that paper to sign her over. The lawyer was so amazed because the Social Welfare Department rang and said could they please have Suzie's milk for her.

'I said, "I've just finished breast-feeding her."

'My lawyer just sort of look at me then and said, "Oh no. That doesn't seem right . . . you realise that's not right." I don't think he wanted to do anything, didn't want to proceed any more. And he sort of suggested, "Why don't you do the right thing — get her father to pay for what he did?"

'"It's not that easy . . . he's married."

'He said, "It doesn't make any bloody difference . . . Maybe you should go for what you deserve."

'"I don't want to hurt his wife, because we actually know each other and I feel . . . I just want to leave it alone." And right up to today I'm still glad I didn't do anything,' Patricia adds. 'Of course I blamed him, and everything, hell yes. But I knew nothing would come out of it. Some months later I was having a meal with my sister, it was kind of to help me get over things because she understood what I was going through, and he saw

me in the bar. I'd had a few drinks and abused him terribly
. . . he said he didn't know I was pregnant . . . I hadn't told him.

'After I'd signed the adoption paper and went home I felt a
terrible sense of loss. I'd actually met Suzie's adoptive parents for
a few minutes, but I was very upset and I didn't really say anything.
There were thousands of things I was going to say to them, but
I didn't know I had a right to say anything . . . I wanted to say,
"If we could keep in touch," and that, but . . .' Patricia stops in
mid-sentence for a few seconds, the memories still weighing
heavily on her, '. . . they didn't say I could say anything so I
thought I couldn't ask for too much because I felt I should be
grateful to even meet them. I know now I had a perfect right to
meet them. I know her mother is a Maori like me and her father
is a Pakeha, and that she has a brother, and when I applied for
her non-identifying information I found out that they came from
Hastings, so presumably she's up there. I would love to see her
— it's my biggest wish. I've thought about trying to contact them.
I was going to do that this year, but I would really like to be at
peace of mind within myself first — and I realise there's quite a
bit of work involved in looking for her. Also I didn't realise that
it was okay to try and trace her, I thought it was actually illegal
and I'd be doing something really bad. I don't want to do anything
that's going to be going around the back way, because I think all
my life things have been back to front and I want to approach
things more honestly now. I'm prepared to stand back if I have
to rather than causing myself too much trouble and causing too
much trouble for her.'

About a year ago Patricia heard of an adoption support group
in her area and decided to find out what it was all about. She
has been attending the meetings regularly since then and has
found the support invaluable. She also learnt that it was not
illegal to attempt to trace her daughter, who was born in 1975,
and that the Social Welfare Department has a policy of releasing
non-identifying information to both birth mothers and adult
adoptees.

'I'd had about ten years of sheer hell within myself,' she says,
'and so when I heard about the group I thought I'd go because
they said you could identify with other people in the same situation

— I thought that's the bloody place I need to be because all the things I was wanting to say were just sitting in there. I couldn't say them to people who didn't know my situation, and I even find it hard to talk about it with my mother because she doesn't want to talk about it, so a lot of things just stayed in there and I became really angry inside. It has helped tremendously talking to other women. I stopped blaming myself . . . I used to say things like, "I hope I get punished and not Suzie, and that she had gone into a nice home." I used to put a lot of punishment onto myself and I felt I didn't want to have any more children, I didn't feel worthy of it. I think I've stopped blaming other people for my situation now — I blamed my mother and father, I blamed the world, God, anything I could think of, I blamed them all. But I've sort of come to terms with it myself. At the time I felt safe going through with the adoption, even though I wasn't aware of all the grief I was going to feel — no one counselled me or anything like that.

'I also felt I was like my real mum, because when I was little they labelled her as bad and when I gave up Suzie I actually felt those words come back to me — kind of "like mother, like daughter". They all came back and I actually took all those labels upon myself and felt really bad and awful inside — and I thought, gee, now they've got something to say because I am very much like her. I've thought about it all a lot since then. I can understand my mother having me and then giving me up for a better life — that's what I understand I was given up for — because they were poor and my adopted mum and dad, they're not rich, but they're comfortable and have given me all the nice things. I don't know what I would be like if I'd stayed with my mother. I look at my real sisters and they're all so mixed up and everything, they don't lead very good lives. In some ways I'm grateful to my adopted mum and dad because I was given guidelines for different things, and that's something they weren't given. But they do radiate a lot of love, a lot of personal love, which is kind of different to me because I feel people have to do something to get my love — I don't really mean that — but that's the way I sometimes put things across to people. I mean like how my parents say, "You got the best, a private school and all that."

Also, I think my real brothers and sisters envy me a lot. They say, "Your life wasn't as bad as ours, you shouldn't have gone so crazy, you shouldn't have made so many mistakes." They feel they've got reasons to make mistakes, and with me I shouldn't have made quite so many. But I believe I was destined to make those mistakes myself — nobody makes you.

'I've got really close to my real mother now, because my adopted mother has only got about three to six months to live and I feel that without her I'll really have nobody. And I've been learning a lot of things from my real mum — like she said that when I was a little girl she used to come and visit and want to hold me and kiss me, put dozens of kisses on me, and she just held back because she didn't feel she could. I also found out how my twin sister died — they were really poor and they couldn't get her to the doctor in time. And I know now that my real mother isn't bad. I found out for myself that they forgot to say that she's a real sensitive, loving lady. These are things that some people might consider quite trivial but are really important to me.

'For a long time I didn't fit in anywhere. I tried to identify myself as a Maori, tried to understand my life, but even though I had a good education, I couldn't be white, and I couldn't really be a Maori either because my Dad brought me up to get away from all that. And I found out they changed my name — Patricia is really my middle name — I s'pose it was their way of covering up who I really was. But these things are all going to come out eventually — I can't get away from the fact of what I am!' Patricia laughs, pointing to her dark brown skin and Maori facial features. 'But it's really nice because I'm now learning about all sorts of things that are Maori and I really love it. It's important and I felt that in some ways I was denied my right to know who I am and what I am.'

Patricia remarried five years after Suzie's birth and, with her new loving and supportive husband, had another child. 'I think that's when my life straightened out a bit,' she says. 'He's a beautiful baby and I loved having him. I thought I would go through it not wanting to know him, but right from the time I knew I'd conceived I talked to him every day and told him he was safe — I'm now happy about myself as a mum.

'My children think it's bloody brilliant to have two sets of grandparents — heaps of presents coming in on birthdays and at Christmas time! And heaps of aunties. They think it's all good fun, they really thrive on it, and I think it's really good. And I've slowly told them that they have another sister too. It wasn't difficult but the hardest part was when they said, "Why did you give her away?" I said, "That was really hard, but at the time I'd separated from your dad and was having a lot of trouble financially, and I just couldn't cope." They're pretty good, because they actually accept that. I've made it as open as I can and they're looking forward to meeting their half-sister — and I'm quite confident that will happen in the future. If it doesn't happen between now and when she's twenty I'm quite confident she'll look for me. I've also put a note on my files at Social Welfare that should I die I want her to know that, and that I thought about her all the time . . . there's hardly a day goes by when I don't think of her and pray for her, and wonder where she is and if she's happy in her life.

'I'm surprised Suzie's mother hasn't felt something. She's a Maori but she might be like me, and it's just recently that I've realised that's important to me. I've wondered whether she might be one of these ladies who thinks it's important for tribal reasons for Suzie to get to know who she belongs to. I think the main thing about adoption is your identity — to be able to hold on to it, like have a genetic right to know who you are, or biological, whatever they like to call it — so long as you didn't lose your identity.'

SIX

The opportunity was there: David

David grew up knowing both he and his sister were adopted. They both had a happy and stable childhood and were encouraged to use their minds to gain university degrees. At twenty-seven he is now the Wellington branch manager for an international company. He and his wife Shenaigh lead a comfortable life and are definitely 'upwardly mobile'. Six months ago David decided to trace his birth mother. They have since met and formed a warm and close friendship. He has no desire to make contact with his birth father.

'I've always known I was adopted. I can't remember being told but I can remember it being spoken of a number of times, though I'd always known before that,' David begins, taking a sip of the chilled white wine he has graciously poured into crystal glasses. 'Mum would occasionally talk about how fortunate it was that she and I were so alike given that I was adopted, which was very true. The only explanation I remember is that my parents couldn't have their own sons or daughters — they never said babies, I was never spoken to in baby talk — and so they went *looking* for some and *chose* me. Mum coped with any thoughts that I might resent being adopted by turning it into a positive thing: "With most parents they just get what they're landed with but we went out and said, yes, we'll have *that one*." I always felt quite good about that — like being off the top shelf of the Harrods baby department!

'I was told I was adopted at the age of two weeks from Childhaven in Auckland, that my mother had specifically asked for me to be brought up Anglican — now that's not actually true, my birth mother doesn't remember doing that and her family are

Presbyterians, so it's unlikely. I was told that my father was six foot four and wore glasses — I've since found out he wasn't six foot four. I was told that my mother was a student. I automatically assumed university student but she was a student teacher. I also knew her name was Jillian Catherine Goodwin — the secrecy leaked like a sieve! But I was never certain that was her name. I can't remember being told it, but I can remember it being mentioned when we lived in Taylor Street, I was seven when we moved, but I don't think it was the first time I was told.

'The other thing I can remember, I must have been very young — probably no more than four or five — is my father tucking me into bed one night and I said to him, "You're really very nice to me considering I'm not your real son." I can clearly remember that because the next day I was told how hurt he was. Of course as an adult now I can see why he was hurt, but at the time I didn't mean it to hurt, I meant it as a thank you.'

David's parents split up when he was fourteen. He had never been particularly close to his father, and living with his mother and sister in a different town until he went to university widened the gap. He analyses it: 'I think my parents' unhappy marriage caused Dad to retreat from the whole family situation anyway. He died when I was twenty and I had become much closer to him just before then, but it was less a father-and-son relationship by that stage. He was a nice man, a good man, but he and my mother weren't suited and she would freely admit that.

'I never worried about being adopted. If anything, it made me a little unique and in a way I was quite proud of it. I dare say on occasions I proudly told people I was adopted when my mother would have preferred I didn't . . . even now she would be reluctant for some of her friends to know, not perhaps close friends, but acquaintances, because there's still an element in her that feels — she probably wouldn't agree but I think it's still true — that she failed because she couldn't have children. She thinks she's only ninety-nine per cent a mum and that had she had her own children she would have been a hundred per cent. Although we have our ups and downs now, I would think that till I grew up she was more like a hundred and fifty per cent a mum. Also she's always been very good about adoption. When

I was sixteen or seventeen she wrote to Jigsaw and said that she, as the adopting mother, had no objection if either my sister Vicki's natural parents or mine wanted to make contact with us. The only slightly negative thing, and it really only pisses me off now because I don't remember it when I was young or even a teenager, is that since I was about eighteen or so, and she and I have had some fairly personal disagreements and have really grown in very different ways, every now and again she says, "I just wonder if we wouldn't have these fights if you'd been my natural child." It pisses me off when she says it, but it doesn't worry me long term, because to her credit she didn't do it till I was well old enough to be able to understand and can just walk away from it and say, "This is nonsense, I'm sure I'd disagree with you anyway, you silly woman!"

'I always had this image of my birth father being a tall, bespectacled, respectable lawyer type of man, probably with a deep voice and extremely rich!' David smiles. 'In other words, it was everything I wished I was, a projection of my own self-image . . . and possibly a compensation factor, in that Dad never really wielded much influence over me.'

But while David's adoptive mother was open to her children making contact with their birth mothers, as a teenager David was not interested and never pursued it. He says he was a little curious, but that the only time he gave any serious thought to what his birth parents were like was when he was angry with his adoptive ones, and it was not in the context of trying to trace them.

Then, in September 1986, when David was twenty-six, the Adult Adoption Information Act came into effect. He had not been following its progress closely but had seen the newspaper stories and was pleased to read it had been passed. Two months later he applied for his original birth certificate, which confirmed the name he had grown up knowing. Jillian Catherine Goodwin was twenty-one and living in Auckland when she gave birth to David. No name was in the space provided for the father.

'There was no great excitement or anything,' he says, 'but then I already knew most of what was on the certificate and I'd applied for it out of a sense of curiosity combined with opportunity, rather than any pressing need. The timing was because I was unhappy at work, I was bored, and because I'd been talking to a friend who had just discovered her natural family. The subject had come up, so I thought, oh well, this might be interesting, and ordered the birth certificate — and then I sat on it for about six months. One day I was off sick and had dropped Shenaigh off at work and decided to drive through town rather than along the motorway because I wasn't in any great rush, and I drove past Levin House [where national birth, death and marriage records are held] and thought, oh that's where I'd have to go — well let's go and have a look. It was as simple as that, as random as that. I hadn't worked up the courage, I hadn't sat there thinking about it, I just happened to pass Levin House and thought, fine, seeing as I'm here I might as well stop in.

'At any one time they're prepared to search five or six years — so I said, "Two of those years you can allocate to looking for her birth certificate" — from her age on my birth certificate she had to have been born within a limited range of months — "and use the remaining ones for her marriage certificate from 1960." And sure enough, they found the birth certificate and the wedding certificate just like that. It was dead easy. On the wedding certificate [dated 1961] I found that she had given her home address in Auckland and I figured that was probably her parents' address. I phoned Shenaigh at work — she grabbed the Auckland phone book and looked for a Goodwin at that address, and sure enough there was still one there, and it had her father's initials. It had to be the same. At this I was feeling excited because I was starting to find things, like tracking down a big story on a newspaper, this was marvellous! And it was all so quick and easy. Shenaigh also looked up the name P. A. Allen [Jillian Goodwin's married name] and there were two, so I s'pose I could also have tracked her down that way.

'I had to tell someone, I was excited about it, and I went to see the friend I'd talked about it with before. We had coffee, talked for a while and then I went home and tried to write a letter to my grandfather, James Goodwin, explaining who I was, and then decided, to hell with it, I'll phone, I've got this far, why wait? It was engaged so I phoned Shenaigh again a couple of times, and had another read of the letter and thought, well maybe I should send it, but then I decided, bugger it, I will phone. And I just knew it was going to be all right to phone. I had no doubts, I don't know why, I just knew it. I'd never had that sense of certainty until I went to Levin House and found that contact address and from then I knew that everything was okay, that I wasn't going to cock up her life, that this wasn't going to be rejection, that it was all going to be a wonderful thing.'

David had planned exactly what he was going to say and overcame any nervousness by rehearsing his lines again carefully. He dialled the Auckland code and then the number for the second time. The phone rang and was answered by an elderly woman, his grandmother.

'Mrs Goodwin? Good afternoon, my name is David Gray. I'm calling from Wellington . . . I'm attempting to locate Jillian Catherine Goodwin and I understand she may be your daughter?' There was a pause in the conversation, then David continued, 'I should explain to you why I'm calling . . .'

'Yes,' Mrs Goodwin acknowledged, already almost certain of the reason for David's call.

Sensing the meaning behind the 'yes', he continued, 'I am twenty-seven years of age, and I was adopted by my parents from Auckland in 1960. My birthday's the fourteenth of May . . . I've recently obtained my birth certificate and it says on it that my mother was Jillian Catherine Goodwin. I've since located her marriage certificate, which gives this address as her home address and I guessed that might be her parents' . . . hence I'm calling you.'

'Isn't it amazing how much you can find out about people from the records,' Mrs Goodwin responded, adding, 'Well yes, we've been wondering if we'd get a call.'

'The reason I'm phoning you is that I don't wish to barge into Jillian's life unannounced. I don't wish to upset her in any way . . . I'm really just making contact out of a kind of curiosity more than anything . . . it's not something that's so important to me that I would wish it to upset her . . . that's why I'm calling you rather than trying to find her now. I'll go on and try to tell you a bit about myself . . .'

David told his grandmother, known to all her family as Lel, briefly about his life; his wife, adoptive family, education and career.

She then asked, 'Do you resent being adopted?'

'No, I never resented it. I've always known, it's not as though I've just found out, but I'm interested in meeting my birth mother, seeing what we have in common, how much of me is inherited and how much of me is learnt,' David replied, and now adds, 'It was a very wise and shrewd question to ask because if I'd said, "Yes, I do resent it a little", then she would have been able to guess my reasons for contacting Jill were to cause trouble. The analytical side of me has shining admiration for the way she asked that question — we're talking about a woman who is well into her seventies but she's as sharp as a nail. A call like that comes out of the blue, an issue that hasn't been an issue for twenty-seven years suddenly bursts into your living room again and she's still got the smarts to ask that question. That was brilliant. I was really impressed, and I thought, yep, that's my granny! I liked this one — and I knew this one would like me.'

Lel ended the conversation by saying, 'I'm not going to tell you where Jill is . . . please don't do any more looking . . . I'll speak to her.'

'That's fine . . . I'll write you a letter . . .'

As soon as David got off the phone he sat down to rewrite the letter he had written earlier, but this time addressed to his grandmother — in the phone call he had learnt his grandfather had died only months before. He also included photographs of himself.

'I knew they'd want to see that I was respectable,' David says confidently. 'Old ladies are concerned that "the youth of today are never as good as they were", so I just wrote the letter highlighting all the respectable points about me. I told them about my job, the fact that I'd been in the same company for six years, that I had a university qualification, that I was married, stable, no children yet, but two cats! So I made it a very respectable letter, a very polite letter, and I addressed again the question, did I resent being adopted, because I wanted to put that in writing.' David then drove into the city to post the letter from the central mailing service, rather than risk delays at the local suburban post office.

Meanwhile, his grandmother Lel held a quick family conference over the telephone with Jill's elder sisters in Auckland, and then phoned Jill, who, unbeknown to David, was living temporarily in Wellington. Jill's immediate reaction to the sudden news that her son had approached the family and was seeking contact with her was to seek counselling — and that she didn't want any contact at the time but would be happy to see David in the future, when her work contract in Wellington was completed and her life more together. Two days later Lel called Jill again and read out David's letter — the 'respectable' image he presented worked as he hoped it would and Jill immediately phoned him.

'Hello, I'm Jill Allen. I understand you've been trying to get in touch with me.'

'Yes,' David replied as Shenaigh, realising who he was talking with, parked a chair under him.

'We spoke for about forty minutes,' David remembers fondly. 'It wasn't a terribly heavy conversation, it was actually quite chatty and relaxed. We talked about what we were like, found out that we both smoked, found out what I knew of the circumstances. I didn't feel any great emotional upheaval or any great shock, it was a response of intense interest. I s'pose I'd been expecting a call sometime or other, some kind of contact. I knew there would be and it just came quicker than I thought. The emotional response was a far quieter and longer-term thing than that, but then I'm not a particularly emotional person.'

Towards the end of the conversation Jill said, 'Well I suppose we'd better meet.'

'Would you like to have lunch sometime?' David suggested.

'No, let's meet at the weekend . . . come round to my place on Saturday around two o'clock.'

Three days later David was sitting in his car outside Jill's temporary Wellington home. 'I sat there for a couple of minutes just composing myself, taking a few deep breaths. I'd planned what I was going to do in this meeting; we were going to treat this as a very sensible thing, nothing sloppy about it. I was going

to go in and shake her hand. We would sit down and talk about
ourselves, and I'd stay about an hour or so. I'd actually taken a
bottle of wine, two packets of cigarettes, and because she'd told
me she was a teacher I took an apple! This was my joke, my little
flash of humour. I was going to walk in and take out the wine,
take out the cigarettes, and finally "an apple for the teacher". But
it didn't quite work out like that. She lived in a flat underneath
another house and I had to go round the back lawn and up some
steps to a patio, so she actually had the potential to look at me
before I saw her, and I noted that. But I thought, that's okay,
she'll be ready to open the door, she won't jump when I knock,
she'll have composed herself. I walked up the steps and saw somebody sitting in there knitting or reading. My immediate reaction
was, oh she's not blonde, I don't know why but I'd always had
this picture of her as blonde, and she doesn't look very old, but
she didn't. From a distance she could be as young as thirty-five,
and even close up she doesn't look forty-eight. But it wasn't as
though I looked at her and went, "Ugh, you're supposed to be
blonde." It didn't matter and I soon got myself back together from
that and went and knocked on the door — she hadn't actually
seen me coming.

'I said, "Hello, I'm David." She sort of took my hand, she
didn't shake it, and said, "I'm going to give you a hug," and gave
me a big hug. I'm not a touchy-touchy person and I was
expecting more of a sort of careful meeting, where we stepped
carefully and took our time getting close enough to hug. But it
was okay . . . and I finally left her place at eleven o'clock! We'd
been getting on like a house on fire, and I don't think there was
any stress on either part. We just discovered very, very quickly
that we had a lot in common and talked about all sorts of things
like Shakespeare and literature and history. About nine o'clock
she said, "I s'pose we'd better have something to eat. Would you
like me to make you a meal?" And I looked at her and said, "Yes,
that'd be nice, let's face it, it's been a helluva long time since you
fed me!" And she cracked up at that — I wouldn't have said it
if we hadn't have got that far. I came home feeling great, and got
told off for being out so late!'

But while David and Jill spoke mostly about their many

common interests during that first nine-hour meeting, David also learned about the other members of his birth family. He already knew Jill had married about a year after his birth and had correctly assumed her husband was not his father, but he was not aware that he had two half-brothers just several years younger than himself, nor that Jill's marriage lasted for only about five years. She had not remarried.

'Jill explained why I was adopted. She wanted to talk about it but it was a bit painful for her, and it wasn't that important to me, because I always felt she'd done the right thing. For a twenty-one-year-old student teacher in 1960 trying to bring up a child single-handed, no DPB, nothing else, what could she have offered me? And if she'd married the guy because she was pregnant she would never have been happy and I would have been unhappy too. I have no qualms about being adopted and I have no desire for a justification as to why I was adopted. I was interested to know the circumstances because I wanted to get to know Jill and what was going on with her at that time. So it was from that perspective, not a desire to say, "How dare you give me away," that I was interested. Jill wanted to talk to me about it; she felt she owed me an explanation, but that was only partly true, I think rather more she owed herself an explanation. She said she gave me away because there was no way she could give me a decent life — no, that's not true — what she said was that she felt other people would be able to give me a better life. And I think from her point of view my birth was something she had put aside. She was told that it was over, she would forget about it, that it was no longer her child, that it never happened and she should go and start again. She told me she felt a little cheated when the [Adult Adoption Information] Bill went through, and had talked to a few people at the time about me, but equally it was something she never apparently came to terms with because she was simply able to put to one side. She's mentioned about dreams she's had and poems she's written, and that she couldn't understand why she'd dreamt or written them. She thought perhaps she'd written one poem in particular, a lullaby, for Stuart, her fourth son, who died of cancer when he was a child. But after she met me she said she realised she'd actually written it and others for me, because although she lost Stuart, she had evidence of him. I was the baby she had given away . . . I think she's pleased we're in contact,' he says, reluctant to speak directly on her behalf, although the relationship they have formed clearly suggests 'pleased' is a gross understatement.

David and Jill saw each other regularly several times a week over the following three months, then Jill had to return to her life in Auckland. David drove up about two months later to stay with Jill for a week and meet the rest of his new family.

'One of the nice things that happened in Auckland was that my grandmother took me round and showed me Childhaven,' David says. 'We parked outside and I just looked at it for a few moments in silence and Lel turned around and said, "What are you thinking about?" I said, "It's funny to think that two very, very different histories of families converged on this particular location and one of them took away a souvenir of it." I was picturing my mother and father coming to this building to get me, and of all of this, that was probably the single most moving moment for me, the one time I felt a big emotional surge. I knew how Jill got there and I can think of Ray and Nola, my adoptive parents, arriving on the DC3. They've been told that they've got a child — can you imagine the thrill for them getting on that plane and then going into that building? I wasn't born there but I spent the first two weeks of my life there, and just looking at it was quite amazing.'

The visit to Auckland was also the first time Jill felt able to talk about David's father. 'I asked her about my father,' he says, 'though I had no particular desire to know his name or meet him, but the one thing I did want to know was what he did for a job, because I thought I might find in that interesting parallels in me. I can see pretty clearly the kinds of things that I might get from Jill, depending on how much emphasis you put on genetics in this, and if I knew something of him then I could put it into perspective. But that's a little different from wanting to meet him and say, "Hi, I'm your long-lost son." He's probably forgotten about me now, though he knew I existed — it was just a thing that happened. He was apparently a very nice fellow but without much get-up-and-go. Jill's seen him a couple of times since by chance, and the interesting thing is that she now accepts that her family was right in telling her not to marry him. She told me his name, and that he was driving trucks at the time I was conceived and hasn't really done much since. So now I can see that in terms of my inclinations, or talents or interests, I possibly don't have much from him at all . . . but it's not a snobbish thing and I don't look down on him and think, only a truck driver! And in a way I probably feel a great deal of relief, because now I know this fantasy thing wasn't my father after all, and I know it was only a projection of my better thoughts about me. That's fine, I can still be that, whereas had *he* been that, I'd be looking around saying, "Well, I'm not quite a Queen's Counsel, am I!" So I've really done quite well out of that. I know all I need to know and I certainly don't desire contact. Why should I . . . fifteen minutes versus nine months. There's another reason too, and I suspect this is a generation thing to do with the way families were structured in the fifties and sixties, when dads went out to work and mums stayed home and looked after the kids, and therefore the children formed their closest relationships with their mothers. Adopted children who did the same, I think, are still naturally inclined to think in terms of mother when thinking about emotional links, because that's the way it always was. The next generation of adoptees might think differently, although there aren't many of them.'

David and Jill have bridged the twenty-seven-year separation from each other and formed a close and caring friendship. 'I think there are two reasons why we're so close,' he says. 'The first is that Childhaven did a magnificent job for both me and my sister Vicki, because they matched very, very carefully the backgrounds of the children and the people they gave them to. The Goodwins would have been the kind of people my [adoptive] mother and her parents would have felt were good solid citizens with whom we would have been perfectly happy to associate. And because of that matching, any genetic similarity that Jill and I might have had was enhanced because they placed me with parents who developed the talents similar to those Jill would have developed had she been my mother — there was an odds-on bet that Jill and I would have ended up with so many common interests. It was adoption that worked, not just Social Welfare farming children out to the next one on the list. I think the second reason we're so close is that although Jill's forty-eight, she doesn't look it or behave it, and the generation gap is not what you'd expect.

'But I'm no different now than I ever was. The fact that I've met Jill has just brought someone else into my life that I'm very close to, not because she's my genetic mother but because she's Jill. Had we been two strangers meeting, I would have grown just as fond of her but it would have taken longer, because the historical link opened doors and we got through the social aspect quicker and got down to talking about each other a bit more readily than you usually do.

'I don't know where our relationship will go from here. I've been tremendously spoilt because for three months she was here in Wellington and I had her all to myself. I'd be round there a couple of times a week and she was often round here. She's gone now and probably the single toughest thing I've had to face is going up to Auckland and finding she had an entire life up there that I wasn't a part of. There were all these other people who were making demands on her time, who had claims that were greater than mine. But I don't sit back and think, if only she had been my mum for all those years, because I don't feel I ever lacked a mum. I have no desire, no secret fantasy, to re-enter that family situation of mother and son, that's not what I want. What I want is her living down in bloody Wellington so that we can keep on going out together, keep on talking to each other.'

SEVEN

A medical history of my own: Sandy

Sandy decided to trace her birth mother primarily for medical reasons. In her late twenties, and several years before the Adult Adoption Information Bill was passed, she suffered a series of miscarriages and became extremely anxious about the unknown factors in her genetic inheritance. With the help of other adoptees and sympathetic professionals she managed to trace her birth mother and, despite initial difficulties, the two woman now correspond regularly. However, Sandy is fearful of suggesting a meeting in case their delicate relationship is destroyed. She has also not told her adoptive parents anything about the contact.

Sandy and Nigel married when they were in their mid-twenties. They bought a home in a quiet Auckland suburb and began planning their lives in preparation for the large family they both wanted. Four years later, their mortgage manageable and their hire purchase on appliances paid off, Sandy stopped taking the Pill and waited for the first signs of pregnancy. Nothing happened.

'We tried for quite a long time, about a year to eighteen months,' she says, 'and then finally I got pregnant. But I didn't feel right. I'd never been pregnant before but there was something that just wasn't right.' Her premonition was correct and halfway through the pregnancy she began haemorrhaging and then miscarried. The experience left the usually bright and bubbly woman depressed and withdrawn, and her thoughts turned to the fact that she was adopted and had no knowledge of her biological family's medical history.

'I went through this thinking, why am I losing my baby; what's wrong with my family; what is there in my heredity that I don't know about? I could have full brothers and sisters who are hae-mophiliacs, I don't know. Who's got the right to keep this information from me?' she says intensely.

To make matters worse, Sandy miscarried again twice in the same year, each experience adding to her fears about the 'mon-sters' she might produce. For the first time since she was a teenager her adoptive status became a crucial factor in life, and this was compounded by the fact that her adoptive parents were unwilling to discuss the subject. She cannot remember exactly when she was told she was adopted, though it was probably when she was around three or four years old, but she clearly remembers that it was 'very hush-hush'.

'I can remember asking Mum something about adoption when I was quite young, probably about four or five, and her explaining a wee bit,' she says. 'Mum said something about them not being able to have any children of their own and that they went into a hospital to see if they could adopt a baby. She said I was crying, and was the most beautiful baby there, so they didn't even look at anybody else, and I accepted that.

'They were also the sort of parents who said, "The stork brought you," and I believed that for quite a few years. I'm not knocking them, they're not strait-laced or very religious, they're just really conservative and I had a very sheltered life for a long time. The only thing I regret is that they never adopted another child. They said they didn't want another child because I was so happy, and we got on so well that another could have turned out being horrible, but I think the real reason was that they were worried about other people knowing the background. Quite frankly, I don't think that matters, it's irrelevant, and I feel that in some ways not giving me brothers and sisters is affecting my rights. Through the circumstances I'm denied natural half-brothers and half-sisters, and yet they denied me adopted ones as well.

'I used to worry that if anything happened to my parents no one would want me. I get on very well with my cousins and aunts and uncles, and feel like part of the family, but I've always wondered whether they really would accept me if they had to. I also felt that I had to be better than other people because somehow I'd started off not being as good and if I was better it would make up for the fact that I was adopted — which is a load of rubbish,' Sandy adds.

'When I was eighteen I went along to the Births, Deaths and Marriages office one lunch hour and asked for a copy of my birth certificate with the intention of getting my original name. The lady came back to me and said, "You're adopted. You can't have that. Just go away and leave things alone the way they should be." It had taken me weeks to get up the courage to go in and my knees shook when I asked. She was really rude and it took me a long time to get over that. I guess to a certain extent I just felt like I didn't really belong. And I felt illegitimate. My parents had tried to tell me I wasn't, that my parents had been married and had separated, but I don't think I believed it. In those days illegitimate children were scum — I didn't believe that, but it did make me feel a little bit tainted.

'I've tried two or three times to talk to Mum and Dad about searching for my birth mother but they don't want to discuss it. They feel threatened, and clam up and get very embarrassed. My mother looks as though she's about to burst into tears, and my father's apt to walk out of the room. It's just not worth it. Mum said to me once that my birth mother would be a lot younger than her and that I'd find this young glamorous person and wouldn't want little old her for my mother — which is ridiculous. Although your birth mother does mean a lot to you, it's your parents, the ones who brought you up, they're Mum and Dad, and no one would ever replace them.'

But while Sandy was keen to find out about her origins when she was a teenager, as a young adult the desire was overtaken by a busy and full life. She did not forget, but the fact that she was adopted lost its importance — until her miscarriages.

'It was at the time [the early 1980s] when the only people who had got information about their backgrounds were those who had gone through the courts on medical grounds. But I had this marvellous and supportive doctor, and said to him, "If I go through the courts will you give evidence to say my mental health is such that I need to know my medical background?" '

'Yes, I can see you really do need it,' the doctor replied.

Sandy then asked her lawyer, 'Will you take it to court for me?'

'Well, I sympathise with you,' he began, 'and there have been successful cases, but I really don't know what the courts will do . . . you could be in for a very long legal battle. It could be very expensive and you may not get anywhere in the end.'

'We still had heavy mortgages and it just didn't seem worth it,' Sandy says. 'But I resented a system that was so unfair. I could accept the fact that you couldn't know who your birth parents were, but I really felt very strongly that medical information should be available. I didn't want to hurt my adoptive parents by asking them, but after my third miscarriage I felt I had to.'

When Sandy asked for their help, her mother replied bluntly, 'Those things aren't inherited so there's absolutely no point in you finding anything because there's nothing wrong.' And the conversation came to an end.

Sandy had hoped her mother would understand how desperate she was becoming, and was hurt by the apparent lack of feeling. However, she conceived for the fourth time and her pregnancy continued normally. She gave birth to a healthy baby boy. But the questions remained, intensified by the comments of family and friends that her son looked just like her. When he was a year old Sandy began an intensive search for information and finally, through sympathetic contacts, she managed to find out her birth mother's Christian name, then surname, and lastly a middle name. With the help of a friend in Wellington who searched national birth, death and marriage records, Sandy eventually discovered her birth mother, Dorothy, had been twenty-five and single at the time of her birth, married eighteen months later, and now lived in Levin, just north of Wellington.

'Funnily enough, the day I found her was the day I found out I was pregnant with our second child and a friend had a baby — it was quite a day!' Sandy says, still excited by the memory. 'I knew from speaking to other people that the way contact was made was really important and if you got the wrong person handling it you could blow it.'

Sandy asked around the people who had already helped her and eventually found a woman in Wellington, Pauline, who had handled the delicate task before and would act as her go between. But Pauline already had her hands full with her own work and it was several months later when she rang to say she would be going to see Dorothy the next week.

'Before I see your birth mother I just want to make sure you've got the right person,' Pauline checked. 'How did you get her name?'

'I'm sorry but I can't tell you that,' Sandy replied hesitantly. 'It would hurt the people who helped me and cause a hell of a lot of strife — but take it from me it's right.'

'That's fine — I understand. I also wanted to say that I'm not sure how this will go. I've written to Dorothy to say I want to talk about family matters . . . but I think it might be a good idea if you've got someone with you when I call back after I've seen her . . . in case something's gone wrong.'

'I don't know what she was expecting,' Sandy says. 'I think she was worried that she'd get absolutely nowhere and have to come back to me to say she'd found nothing out. When she said I shouldn't be alone my immediate thoughts were that she wasn't very hopeful, so I wasn't hoping for a lot.

'That week — it was like waiting for the results of a pregnancy test! That's the only thing I can liken it to. I tried to keep busy but it's on your mind all day and you're doing your best not to think about it, trying not to think about all the ifs and buts. And as much as I wanted to find her, I was also scared she might want to arrive on my doorstep the next day. I felt I was just opening a can of worms.'

At the end of that long week Pauline's call finally came. Sandy virtually shrieked down the phone, 'Just tell me if it was all right.'

'It went a lot better than I thought it would,' Pauline replied, trying to calm Sandy. 'Your birth mother found it very difficult to talk about . . . it was quite hard going because your adoption was very painful for her . . . she'd just shut it away and hadn't thought about it for thirty odd years . . . it was the only way she could live with it.'

Sandy and Pauline talked for half an hour and Pauline followed the conversation with a letter several days later.

Dear Sandy,
I spent an hour and a half with Dorothy and we had a cup of
tea in the kitchen-dining area . . . your mother has never worked
since she married and sees herself firstly as a loyal wife, mother
and home-maker. She has devoted her spare energy to community work. Her parents died when she was in her teens and,
as there were no other relatives in New Zealand, she found kind
lodgings with a lady in Wellington who was the only person to
know of the unfortunate circumstances of her pregnancy and
was extremely supportive. Her landlady suggested she move to
Auckland for the duration and she did so. She had no means
of support to keep a baby and felt in the circumstances she had
no choice but to place you for adoption. She then returned to
Wellington and took a new position. She's five foot eight inches
tall, plumpish but fit-looking, with grey hair. She had no health
problems during pregnancy, no history of miscarriage, and no
physical deformity in the family as far as she knows. She married
about a year after you were born and never told her husband
about you. She has in fact successfully blocked it out of her mind
over the years and says it was the only way she could deal with
such a painful experience. She has three sons of the marriage,
twenty-eight, twenty-four, nineteen, and a daughter, twenty-
two. I know you'll have further questions and I'll certainly ask
them if the opportunity arises. Let's leave the question of future
contact for the moment when the dust has settled, so to speak.

Good luck.

Pauline

P.S. Since writing this she has now told her husband. He was
kind about it but they both feel they want to leave it at that for
now. She was feeling much better and did not feel the need for
me to visit again.

Sandy replied:

Dear Pauline,
I received your letter yesterday — I'd forgotten a few bits and
pieces you'd told me and it was nice to learn a bit more. Please
keep the photos I sent, as they're not important. I sent them
because I wanted to know if I look like her at all — you didn't
say, but do I look like her?

I was very surprised she told her husband. I really did not think she would. In her circumstances I wouldn't have. I have no intentions of telling my parents about this, despite the possible problems I can see arising in the future. I love them too much to ever chance hurting them. I've given this a great deal of thought and truly feel it would achieve no benefit — this is something Dorothy would need to accept. I really can't understand why she has told her husband now after so many years, perhaps she thought he always suspected. I had been very worried about how she would cope on her own and am pleased to know she can talk to you. I am pleased in a way she told her husband, because obviously she will need support from someone, and I'm relieved he's been kind. I know the whole thing's been very emotional for me, but I have had a lot of time to come to terms with it and believe that now I certainly have no hang-ups about it.

I realise it's a matter of getting on with my life and not waiting for her to possibly want contact. I'm inclined to think that after a period of time, maybe three to six months, she possibly will want to know more about me, especially as her husband, whom I saw to be the main stumbling block, now knows. What do you think, or do you think she will shut the door forever again? I am sure you realise I do not hold anything against her and do sincerely think she did the best thing in the circumstances. I am pleased I have the parents I do and my only regret is being an only child, which of course is not her fault. In my teens I may have felt a bit differently, but now I realise it must have been very hard for her to give me up and feel she was doing the best for both of us. She has no worries about me feeling at all resentful about her. I really can't do anything else to bother her. I, or rather we, don't need or want anything from her other than background and medical information. If she's concerned in that sense, we own our own house and have nothing on HP, and although our existence is fairly modest on one wage, we are well set up as I worked till our first child was born. My parents have brought me up to be very independent and taught me the value of working for what you want, not being given it. Well I must away. I should say to close I do feel guilty feeling so good and settled about my life when my well being has been at the expense of my birth mother's. I feel truly sorry about the difficulties I have caused her — I really didn't think it would upset her so much as I had tried to handle the whole thing as gently as I could.

Thank you again for your invaluable help. I do appreciate it.

Best wishes

Sandy

Sandy tried to be patient as the months passed and she heard nothing more about, or from, her birth mother. On the birth of her second child, this time a daughter, she sent a small letter to Dorothy, through Pauline, to let her know she had a second grandchild. Three months later, still without any further news, Sandy began considering writing directly to her birth mother. But before she had made a decision a letter arrived from Pauline with the following note enclosed.

> Dear Pauline,
> I have given a great deal of thought about what to do about Sandy. I have talked it over with my husband and we agreed it would be the best thing not to have any further contact. I return the photographs and I do not wish to see you again. I wish the matter to drop.
>
> Dorothy

Pauline added:

> Dear Sandy,
> I was rather astonished to find the enclosed letter in the mail today. As I told you on the phone, your birth mother seemed quite welcoming for me to visit her, but maybe her husband has influenced her in some way, or maybe it was after I left that she thought things over and felt more uneasy than she realised. I know she is very concerned about her children, whether to tell them about you and how they would react. Whatever the reason, I feel very disappointed by this letter, yet I know what I feel can only be a tiny percentage of the hurt you will feel from this. I am truly sorry. I shall be thinking of you.
>
> With warmest wishes
>
> Pauline

'I didn't take it very well,' Sandy says softly, still visibly upset by the memory. 'I cried, but I wasn't angry. I just felt very, very sorry that she was so scared, because I felt that our relationship could only be of benefit to both of us. I was also worried that she had got the wrong impression, that she was scared I was just going to arrive on her doorstep and cause trouble, or tell her children, and I just wouldn't do that. I'd found out that she was happy but I wanted to tell her that I was happy, that I was pleased she hadn't had an abortion, that she might have gone through some pain but it wasn't just a waste — I appreciated what she had given me. So I decided that as we had got absolutely nowhere all I could do was sit down and write to her . . .'

Dear Dorothy,
I have just received Pauline's letter and your letter to her regarding me. While I never intended to contact you myself in any way, your attitude to me is such that I feel I have to say a couple of things before we both shut the door on our past and bury it forever. First and foremost, I never intended to hurt you in any way — this is why all my contact has been through a third person. It would have been so much easier to have done it myself instead of getting everything second hand, but I respect the right to privacy and it was only that you seemed to think so badly of me that has prompted me to try and write this. This is the most painful thing I have ever had to do but feel that I have to describe your apprehensions. I did not want you to take the place of my mum. As corny as it sounds, I had hoped to think of you as a friend. I had wonderful caring parents, whom I adore, and I will always be eternally grateful you gave me up for adoption. I would not have wanted it any other way. However, it was important to me that you knew you had done the right thing, as many birth mothers often lived the remainder of their lives wondering if what they did was best. It was. I have wanted you to know something of my life, after all you gave it to me, and when you give someone something so valuable you hope it has been worthwhile. I do hope I have lived up to your expectations. It is important to me, especially now when I know something of the difficult circumstances you were in, that you feel you did not give birth in vain. My children give me so much joy, love and pleasure in my life I feel guilty that I have given nothing to you.

I wish that I'd never started this long and painful search. I truly did not intend to cause you further pain. I had hoped to offer friendship and understanding in exchange for a little knowledge. I knew you would not want to tell your family, friends, etc. of my existence and as far as I am concerned I never will. I do not want my parents to know I know about you for exactly the same reasons. I understand the situation completely, but I had hoped to find out about you as a person, how much of me is heredity and how much is a product of environment.

If I have any further miscarriages I will no longer worry about giving birth to an abnormal child owing to hereditary problems, because I know now there is nothing to worry about. I would still like to know lots of silly things like: Is your hair curly? When did you go grey? Do you bite your nails? Do you find it almost impossible to keep your weight down? Are you artistic? (I am.) I didn't realise my silly little questions, so important to me, would be so upsetting to you. I am very grateful for the little information that has been relayed to me. I know now that if I pass someone in the street who looks like me, it won't be you, because you don't live here. However, I would still like to know if I bear any resemblance to you. I would still dearly appreciate a photo.

Please forgive me for disrupting your life. I really have tried not to cause more pain. I had hoped that you might, even in a limited way, want to receive what I had to offer, friendship, and I feel very badly that obviously the best decision for you is to lose me once again. Should you ever change your mind I will in the foreseeable future keep Pauline informed of my current address.

Please forgive me.

Sandy

'It took me several goes and gallons and gallons of tears to write the letter. I was really trying to let her know how I felt,' she says. Without pausing, she then picks up the letter that arrived several weeks later, and with great joy reads sections of it:

Dear Sandy,
First of all I'd like to thank you for your thoughtfulness and understanding in writing to me, which I did appreciate, and now I feel there is no misunderstanding between us . . .
I thought it was better for you to be adopted and have the

security of a home, which I felt I could not give you. I have been married for many years and have a wonderful husband and four children . . .

I cannot think of you as a child but I will write to you now and again as a friend. I'd like the past dropped and forgotten, as the whole situation was really unfortunate. Your children sound adorable . . .

Regards

Dorothy

It is now two years ago that Sandy received Dorothy's first letter, and the two women have been writing to each other regularly ever since, exchanging photographs and small gifts at Christmas and on birthdays. Sandy now knows she looks very much like her birth mother, and that they have a great many common interests. Their letters have become more chatty and relaxed, both speaking about the daily events in their lives rather than dwelling on the past. Dorothy has also started to end her letters with the word 'love', but their relationship is still fragile.

Sandy has suggested Dorothy might like to telephone her. But the return letter said, 'I think you should leave ringing up — it doesn't bother me but I wouldn't ring you. Writing suits me, but over to you. I told my husband but he said he didn't want it mentioned again and to let it drop, so that is the position.' The words made Sandy wonder whether Dorothy's husband even knew about their letters, and she doesn't like to ring in case new problems arise.

Sandy would also like to know about her birth father, even though he probably isn't aware of her existence, but is afraid such questions may destroy the delicate relationship with Dorothy.

'She's told me a little bit about my father — where she met him and what his occupation was — but I guess I've accepted the fact that I'm just not going to know much. I'd like to know about him, but for me to push it and try to find out about him, not only do I risk damaging the relationship with her, but what little she may be able to tell me is not worth losing a hell of a lot for. Her pain is more important than my curiosity. I know it wasn't a permanent relationship and so she may well have forgotten, I don't know. Do birth mothers forget?'

And the future? 'For now I'm quite content to continue writing,' Sandy says, 'though I'm always worried that she might say she doesn't want to write any more. But I would like to meet her one day — I'd jump on a plane tomorrow if she'd agree to meet me — but I don't mind if I have to wait five, ten, twenty years. I've thought about writing and saying, "I know you don't want any direct contact but will you at least agree to meet me before you're eighty?" But I don't think I can. I don't know. I'm scared that by suggesting things I might hurt her or put her off.'

Although the future relationship between Sandy and Dorothy is still uncertain, and there have obviously been times of pain for both of them, Sandy is certain that the bond between them is growing stronger. She has no regrets about making contact, despite the initial problems and the growing difficulties in keeping it a secret from her adoptive parents.

'Dorothy's letters bring me great joy and real acceptance and knowledge of myself,' she says. 'I think the biggest difference is that whole time I was carrying our first child I had visions about the monster I might produce. With our second child I knew I had nothing to worry about. Our first child is very highly strung and a very sensitive little boy. When I was pregnant with our second child I was reasonably happy the whole way through, and our daughter is very confident and very sure of herself.

'I guess I've also accepted myself. They talk about adolescence in terms of trying to find yourself and all those trendy sayings, and I went through that more so because I was adopted and didn't know who I was to begin with. Now I've found out who I am, I know my faults but I'm not trying to make myself into somebody else. So much of me has come from Dorothy — I've turned out as her daughter, not my adoptive parents' daughter, though I am their daughter in so many respects. I've got acceptance of myself because I can identify with her instead of seeing things in myself that were totally alien to my adoptive upbringing and thinking, what's wrong with me, what have I done wrong, why don't I fit in?'

EIGHT

Unreal expectations: Elizabeth

Elizabeth Norfolk was born in New Zealand in 1967, but lived in Africa from the time she was several months old until she was fifteen, when her family moved to Britain. She grew up knowing she was adopted, and with the encouragement of her adoptive father, a New Zealand-born academic, searched for and subsequently met both her birth parents. However, while contact was initially welcomed by both parents, there have been many difficulties since those first meetings.

Elizabeth is a calm and confident young woman who seems older and more mature than her years suggest. She speaks with a distinctly upper-middle-class English accent, and makes polite conversation while preparing jasmine tea (her suggestion) for her visitor. Sitting in the sun room of the charming turn-of-the-century wooden villa, her grandmother's home in Christchurch, Elizabeth explains that her adoptive parents, both New Zealanders, were living in Africa when they decided to adopt a daughter. They returned to New Zealand for six months, adopted her, and the family then went back to Africa.

'When I was two my mother died and my dad was left with an eight-year-old, my older brother, a two-year-old, me, and a one-year-old, my younger brother,' she says with a touch of sadness in her voice. 'It was a very difficult time for him but he's been a wonderful father, and, being in Africa, we had an *ayah*, a nanny. When I was about fifteen we went over to England.

'I grew up knowing I was adopted . . . I think children when they're small ask "How was I born?" and all that sort of thing. I was always told I had another mummy but I was very much wanted, and in fact having another mummy made me more wanted by my adoptive family. Obviously for a long time it didn't mean anything, but it slowly dawned on me what it was, and it's never been any problem. I never really thought about seriously setting out to find my birth parents, but my father has always really encouraged me. He's an incredibly intelligent man and realised it was a good idea, and I think it is too. I can remember when I was about twelve and visiting New Zealand, my grandmother said, "Maybe next time you come out you can look up your parents," and I can remember thinking, do I really want to? But Dad's always thought it's an important part of life to try to find out your identity, and I think I agree with him. So it's sort of grown. When I was nineteen, and had finished school and was ready to travel, I wrote to my gran and she started the process by going to see the Social Welfare Department. My dad came out when it was all going on and he had to sign papers — I'm not quite sure of the procedures — it was before the [Adult Adoption Information] Bill came in, but I was treated as a special case because I only came out to New Zealand for a short holiday and wasn't going to be here when the Bill went through. I came out in November 1985 — everyone was telling me it could take years to find my birth parents and I could be really disappointed — but it all happened in only about three weeks, which was amazing!

'The department was marvellous,' Elizabeth says. 'They traced my natural mother, Jocelyn, who was up in Nelson. The social worker rang her and she really wanted to see me, in fact I talked to her on the phone first and then drove up to Nelson to meet her. It was really strange because it all seemed very natural. I was nervous before we met, but it just sort of slid along and happened. We didn't actually meet for very long, a few hours, but afterwards I was utterly exhausted. We talked about what had happened to her and the way she felt very emotionally distraught about having to go and sign the adoption papers after I was born, giving up all rights to me. She was crying when she was telling me this — the wounds were still there.

'We also talked about her family . . . she didn't really talk much about my birth father, Rob, but she told me they were both English and came out to New Zealand separately. They met and had a fling, as it were, and she got pregnant — I thought my birth parents must have been very young but she was thirty-one and he was twenty-nine. He said, "Yes, I'll marry you. Will you move in with me?" Which she did, but after a short while she realised things weren't going to work out so she came down to Christchurch and had me — and then the Norfolks adopted me.

'We parted on really good terms, I thought, and I said I'd get in touch when I came through Nelson again. I wasn't going to be going up that way for a couple of months so I didn't contact her and presumed everything was okay. Then suddenly I got this irate phone call from Social Welfare, saying, "Your mother's been in contact with us and she's absolutely out of her mind because she thinks perhaps you don't want to see her any more." I rang her up immediately and she really told me off. I organised to go and see her and it was terrible. Oh God, it was awful. Everything I said she would contradict — she was very, very rude to me and said things like, "If only I'd known I was pregnant earlier than three months I would certainly have had an abortion." It really made me feel unwanted, and I went through a time of feeling I never wanted to see her again. In my family I've always felt incredibly wanted, but I'd always been told by my father that my birth mother really wanted me but couldn't have me, and that I was a child of love. So when she started saying all these things I felt very, very rejected and terrible, awful.

'I think it was basically a misunderstanding . . . I'd gone into the whole thing fresh and open-minded, whereas she'd had the experiences of the last twenty years. And I think she showed so much anger towards me because I made her think about it, reminded her about Rob. She had all those emotions to cope with, whereas I just had the meeting. I presumed everything was okay, but she was much more sensitive to it than I was.'

Elizabeth, deeply hurt by her birth mother's words, was desperately looking forward to returning to England, where her adoptive father and brothers were living. Shortly before flying home she asked Social Welfare to get in touch with her birth father, who lived in Wellington and was easy to trace because of his business connections. Then she changed her mind because of the experiences with her birth mother. Elizabeth spent the last few days of her visit to New Zealand with a friend in Wellington. The day before she was due to fly home her friend suggested she ring Rob.

'No, I can't,' Elizabeth reacted. 'I've got to get someone else to ring him. I don't want to.'

'You're going back to England tomorrow, he's staying here, so it's not as though you'd be imposing . . . just the satisfaction of having rung him,' the friend said.

Elizabeth decided to take the advice. 'In a way one of the reasons I wanted to ring him was just to make him realise he'd missed out on so much over all those years,' Elizabeth explains, hastening to add, 'It's spiteful and immodest because you're really saying, "Look at this wonderful person you missed out on!" I felt very bad about ringing him because I don't think it's fair just imposing yourself like that, but I was leaving the next day, so I thought, why not? I rang him at work, it was about lunchtime, and my heart was just going like mad . . .

' "Is that Rob Ferguson . . . I'm terribly sorry to disturb you like this but I'm leaving New Zealand tomorrow and this is the last chance I have to talk to you. You don't know me but my name is Elizabeth Norfolk and my birth mother is called Jocelyn . . . and I believe you knew her some years ago?"

' "Oh God! What was her last name?" Rob exclaimed.

' "I don't know her maiden name . . . she's married now."

' "Oh God! I really want to meet you . . . I'd love to see you and I don't care whether you've got one arm or one leg, you're my daughter and that's what matters."

'It was incredible how he reacted,' Elizabeth says. 'He was marvellous. He said, "Come round and see me — but I've got to tell my wife first." At this point I thought I should step out of it, but he told her and she was wonderful. So I saw him and then went back to England the next day. It was all terribly emotional because he was writing and saying, "You must come and live with us, you must come and work in the family business with us." He rang me once or twice a week and I got letters from him all the time. He was so receptive, so welcoming and loving — it was wonderful! And so finally I decided to go and live with him.

I didn't really want to at first, but it was me coming out to New Zealand to see him — I wasn't obligated — but it was assumed I would. I was very worried about having space and I didn't want to put myself in a situation I couldn't handle, and I knew it would be a very emotional time. Anyway it ended up that he'd got a bedroom ready for me and my own study, so six months after we first met I came back.'

While in England Elizabeth, encouraged by her adoptive father, also wrote to her birth mother, and once back in New Zealand she began ringing her regularly every two to three weeks. 'It's taken a long time but we've now got a good relationship,' she says. 'Jocelyn said afterwards she realises that when we first met, and for quite a long time, she felt so alien towards me because after nineteen years she'd been able to forget it all — suddenly I came along and opened up the wound again. She was made to think about it, and I was the key to a lot of sadness and unhappy memories. A lot of bitterness and anger and resentment came out, and there was no one to direct it against but me. And it was partly me as well — after we first met I wrote saying perhaps I could come and spend my birthday with her and she wrote back saying yes. Then I said, "Oh, I'm spending it in Christchurch." I didn't think it would be hurtful but apparently it was. Now she keeps apologising, and said in one of her letters, "Now the caring can begin." It's really lovely. I've seen her three times now — we'd never had any physical contact but this last time we sort of kissed when I left. She wrote to me and said she was dying to give me a big hug, and I was dying to give her a big hug! I'd like to get to know Jocelyn more now, in a way to get to know more about me.'

But Elizabeth's relationship with her birth father has worked in the reverse order, and brought with it far more emotional turmoil, from which she is still recovering.

'Rob has apparently always wanted a daughter,' she explains. 'When his wife, Chris, was pregnant with their son Jamie, who's ten now, he was quite sure it was going to be a girl. Chris says that when she thinks about it now it was quite unnatural — he was obsessive about having a daughter and when Jamie was born she felt like saying "put him back" — which is terrible. So when

I came back out here — that was only about ten months ago — he thought it was wonderful. He introduced me to all his friends as "my daughter Elizabeth". We went to all sorts of places together and did all sorts of things, not just him and me, but as a family. Jamie thought it was wonderful having a sister, and I love him, and Chris's been wonderful. But then we got over the honeymoon stage and got down to living, and everything wasn't so rosy,' Elizabeth says, the words beginning to tumble out rapidly.

'He started abusing me, not physically, but saying things like I epitomised all the worst aspects in British society he despises most, those were his exact words, and that I'm lazy, a useless lump, and that he was terribly disappointed in my coming out here because I hadn't taken advantage of all the opportunities he'd given me. And he thought it was terribly selfish the way I referred to my dad and family — I couldn't believe this. It was terrible.

'I stayed there from January through to April. Over a week or so you could tell something was wrong because he'd be tense and very short-tempered, and suddenly he'd come out with it all and blow me up — and then he'd say, "I'm so sorry, I don't know what came over me." But it's like an alcoholic, he'd say that and then a few days later he'd do it all over again. He'd think about something for quite a long time and so he'd build it up in his mind. I'd be in tears, I'd cry for nights, I'd just cry myself to sleep. I went and talked to a social worker, which really helped, but Rob refused to talk to anyone, so he'd build this all up in his mind and work out his argument. He's a very stubborn person — he said to me once, "You're so stubborn, Elizabeth, I really don't know where you get it from." Elizabeth manages to laugh, although the memories are still fresh and painful.

'I wanted to leave but I was in a situation that was so important, and I also didn't want to because of Jamie, my half-brother. I felt it would be unfair on him and I really wanted it to work out for him, so I stayed much longer than I would have otherwise. Chris was coping very well — she was caught in the middle but she was incredible the way she welcomed me. She went through stages of thinking, "If she's really a daughter it should be our daughter," and feeling let down, but she's a really understanding and lovely person.

'I've tried to analyse it all and I think basically it comes down to the same as any parents and children, and having a relationship, what role do they play? With Chris, my stepmother, my role is very clear: she's my stepmother. With Jamie it's very clear: he's my half-brother, and you can have a number of brothers and sisters. But you can only have one real father and one real mother, and it's this whole thing of what role does Rob play? I've had a very close upbringing to my father because he's a single parent and because we're a very close family and get on very well. And so yes, I did refer to my dad often, and Rob thought this was selfish of me, but he can't be my father really; he is my father and yet he's not. He'd take me around and introduce me as his daughter, and yet I'm not his daughter and he's not my father — it gets terribly confusing.

'Basically the expectations of me were really stacked very high when I came out to New Zealand — I was his newly found daughter. He admitted this. He said that because I'd been in England for so long and we'd been writing and talking, he'd built up this whole fantasy which he now realises is totally unrealistic. He had images of us flying around the country together, him sharing all his old haunts, going places together, and setting up in the business together. But I was a different person from what he thought a daughter should be, and I wasn't what he wanted. I had a very different upbringing from the one he's giving his son. I've developed as a person and I'm not a child to shape as he wants. Obviously I'm still young and can be moulded, I'll develop more, but the basics are there. I knew I wasn't the person he thought I was, and I knew he wasn't the person I thought he was. The person I'd met in the letters and phone calls just didn't prepare me for the person I met in the flesh. He was completely different . . . and the thing is, it's really sad because through all of this he was trying so hard, he was obviously trying. He wants it to work but he found this whole role business very difficult to cope with, and I think he's very immature and can't deal with his feelings very well.'

Elizabeth finally decided she had had enough, and that she

should leave her birth father's home. 'He had a final go at me and I just broke down crying, I couldn't stop crying,' she says. 'I went up and packed my suitcase. I'd tried to say to him, "Why can't we be friends because I'm friends with my father, why can't we be friends?" He said, "No, we can't be friends, I'm your father. I can't be friends with you," which to me seems very strange.'

As Elizabeth was leaving, Rob again apologised: 'I'm so sorry, it'll never happen again. I don't know what's been happening to me over these last few months, but I feel it's all over now. And will you please forgive me?'

'I said, "Look Rob when I first met you, you had both my respect and my trust and you've lost both of those . . . now you'll have to earn my respect. I just don't trust you, and I don't know whether this relationship is worthwhile at all, it's not worth it to me." And I still feel like that,' Elizabeth adds. 'I used to be a really confident and outgoing sort of person, and he completely drained me of all my confidence and self-esteem and even pride in myself because I kept going back for more and more and more. And it's only been over the last month or so [six months after leaving] that I've started to get my old confidence back. I wasn't myself, and it's a shame because Rob never really has known me — when I first met him I was very tense and nervous, and when I came back out to New Zealand I wasn't myself again. Then just as I was settling down and really relaxing, this all started, so I really wasn't myself.

'When I first met Rob I never compared him to my dad, it never even entered my mind. I thought of them as two different people, but apparently Rob was worried that I would compare them — then I did start to and I was really glad that Dad's my dad. And I also think it's very important for adoptive parents to realise that whatever their children do with their birth parents they should never feel threatened. If they do feel very threatened and have arguments, and try to stop their children looking up their birth parents, they're going to alienate them and it's not worth it in the long run. Dad has always encouraged me — I'm sure he didn't feel threatened intellectually, but emotionally I'm sure he did a bit. In fact he met Rob about three weeks before I came back out here, and he said it was very obvious the expectations were piled so high they had to topple — but he didn't tell me that until afterwards.'

Five months after leaving Rob, Elizabeth decided to make contact with him again, but only by letter.

Dear Rob,
To make contact with you is what I wanted and I'm glad I met you and your family. However, twenty-one years ago you gave up every real chance to have a paternal relationship with me. As a result I've been brought up as the daughter of Harry Norfolk. He gave me an environment full of love and happy family memories. Although you are my genetic father, you rejected the responsibility of being part of the vital years of my childhood, and the development into womanhood. It has become clear to me that family influences are prevalent. They are irreplaceable in creating one's identity and forming family bonding. In our relationship perhaps we are working at cross-purposes — I wanted a friend and you wanted a daughter. I see now that this was unrealistic. Although we all spent time together, your judgment of me seems to be a misconception of my character. I know you have misjudged my value as a worthwhile member of society and even as a person. If we are to have any communication in the future it would only be possible if you were prepared to rethink your attitudes toward the relationship.

All the best

Elizabeth

There has been no reply.

'It's the first relationship I've had with a man, although it's not physical, that's really hurt me. I've always been in control, I've never been hurt, then suddenly I've been incredibly hurt, so it's not easily forgotten,' she says, later adding, 'Perhaps we'll see each other again in the very distant future. I don't feel any need to because I've got my life, he's got his life, and mine is really very involved with my family and he's really not part of my family. I'm glad I met him, yes, but I'm really not concerned about it. I've given him all the chances of respect and trust and love, and he's basically messed all of that up and messed me up in the process. So I feel very angry. Rob said to me, "It's such a pity you did come and stay, because if we'd just seen each other on weekends or kept in touch it would have always been in the honeymoon stage and I wouldn't have said any of those things to you — we'd still be getting on well." But in a way I'm glad I did stay with him, because now I know how he really feels about me and I'm not the daughter he wants.

'But I think finding your natural parents is a very important process for all adopted people to go through, because it's important for your identity to see where you came from. And I think it does give you peace within yourself — even just with practical things like the history of any genetic diseases — it makes you feel happier within yourself. I've always been fascinated by this question of environment versus heredity. Jocelyn says there are lots of things about me that remind her of herself, but I don't really know. My dad doesn't believe your genes contribute to your personality, and in a way I agree. But I've met a couple of Jocelyn's friends who say I remind them of her . . . small things like mannerisms and ways of talking. I don't know whether that's because I look like her or what it is, but I think your basic personality comes from the way you've been brought up, although you can always twist the acts around to suit yourself.

'Knowing your birth parents is also important because you realise that while you may get on with them, it's the people who brought you up who matter, they're your parents, they're your family. And it's no great shakes if you don't get on with your birth parents, because you can look at so many children who don't get on with their parents anyway. The fact that I don't get on with Rob, I've been thinking about it, and I'm really glad he's not my father — even if he had brought me up I'm sure I still wouldn't get on with him! But I just feel much richer for the experience.

'I think that in any situation, however dismal or depressing, you should always try and look towards the future and look at what you've gained from it. And I have gained a lot, even in that every relationship I have in the future hopefully I'll be able to handle it differently and more maturely than how I would have otherwise.'

Elizabeth has since returned to her family in England.

NINE

From every point of view: Gloria

Gloria is in the unusual position of being adopted, a birth mother and an adoptive parent. In the late 1970s she began searching for both her birth mother and the son she relinquished for adoption in 1964. Despite the walls of secrecy at the time, she traced both, but then only to face rejection, anger and denials. Her perseverance, courage and humour over many years finally brought a happy ending to one side of her story. But for the other side she can still only hope.

When Gloria and John married in 1968 the young couple agreed they wanted a large family. Four years later, and with three toddlers of their own, they decided the time was right to increase the family — but this time by adoption. It seemed the natural path to follow. John's brother was adopted, and Gloria was both adopted and a birth mother.

'I wanted to have my own children and I wanted to have adopted ones,' she says. 'I liked children and I wanted to know if it made any difference to my feelings, and it didn't.'

It might seem a strange reason in today's social climate of many childless couples desperately wanting to adopt the small number of babies available, but the late 1960s and early 1970s were the peak time for adoptions in New Zealand.

'We got Trevor in 1972 and Jacqui in 1974,' Gloria continues, 'and they've grown up knowing they're adopted. I told them together when Jacqui was two or three, because she was quite bright and Trevor was a bit backward. I told them they'd come out of a different mummy's tummy and that their mummies couldn't afford to keep them and work too, and that their daddies had gone away. That sort of story. They're part-Maori children and I've found out what I can about their birth parents, told them what they've wanted to know, what their tribes are, what their birth mothers' names are.'

Gloria herself looks part-Maori but her olive skin, dark hair and rounded build are apparently misleading. Like many Pakeha New Zealanders, her ancestors were British. Her marriage to John has since ended in divorce, but she has remarried and describes her new husband Pete, a clerk/messenger with a government department, as a man who was a stranger to adoption but who was quickly educated! The couple have bought a large 1960s house in Wellington's satellite suburb, Wainuiomata, where they live with Gloria's younger children. Gloria is a bright and cheerful woman, often with a cheeky twinkle in her eyes. She is fond of laughter, and with a broad smile, jokes about her 'dirty mind'! Asked her age, she says the year, 1945, rather than a number, but seems younger in both appearance and outlook than the date suggests. She has tried her hand at various jobs and now works in the adoption field, seeming well qualified through her personal experiences.

Sitting at her office desk in the small, tidy but paper-cluttered room she shares with one other woman, she speaks of her adoption experiences in a straightforward and down-to-earth manner, face serious then suddenly alive with the familiar shining smile. The traffic below is distracting for a visitor but Gloria is unperturbed, accustomed to the rumbling that easily penetrates the wall of windows. She speaks confidently, in plain language, choosing to begin her story with the words: 'I was never told I was adopted.' She says them lightly but pauses, loading the sentence with emotion, then continuing without the prompting of a question.

'I was in a choir when I was a teenager, and one night one of the girls said, "You're adopted." I went home and asked my parents but they denied it — and then, behind my back, got hold of the people who had said things and blew them up. I never ever thought of adoption after that but as I grew up, nobody in the family looked like me and I used to ask questions — so they thought I knew but I didn't. I just wanted to know who I looked like. Then, when I was eighteen and working at an insurance company, nosy old me went and looked up a policy my parents had taken out for me when I was a baby. It said, "Parents by Adoption". I was struck dumb. I went into shock for three days, real shock, and just walked around like a zombie. But I knew I wasn't going to get any peace of mind until I'd said something to my parents though I had to be careful because Mum was sick at the time, she was actually dying. On the third night I just went out and put it to them: "Why didn't you tell me I was adopted?"

'Dad just sat there very quietly — I believe he'd wanted to tell me — but Mum, trying to protect me, just didn't know what to say and her eyes filled with tears.

'I said, "Look, it doesn't matter, it's all right, it doesn't make any difference to me," and it didn't.

'Mum said, "Well, there's one thing you should know, at least your parents were married."

'She was trying to protect me as far as being illegitimate was concerned,' Gloria says.

'It was a horrible word in those days, but when I think about it now, it's one of the worst things you could say — some people would take it to heart and think, if my parents were married, why didn't they keep me? But at the time I saw it for what it was, her way of trying to protect me, and I could understand her saying it, though I didn't believe it for a moment.

'I never felt angry with my parents, but I wish I'd grown up knowing I was adopted. I felt there was something different about me, but we were out in the country, there weren't many people around. I was an only child and very protected, and my parents meant well. They never said why they adopted me and I never asked, but I think it was because they'd had two boys of their own whom they'd lost and they couldn't have any more children. I used to nag, "Why can't I have brothers and sisters?" And it got to the point where they said, "You did have a couple of brothers but one died at birth and the other one Mum lost when she had a fall when she was about six months pregnant." So I used to think I had some brothers, but of course they weren't really brothers.

'I was apparently going to be told I was adopted when I turned twenty-one. That was Mum's doing, just wanting to protect me, waiting till I was an adult. She probably thought it would destroy me, knowing before then, but I don't think it would have. When I was a teenager I knew that if I got Dad angry enough he'd just about tell me this secret — Mum would always say, "Tell her when she's twenty-one" — but of course I used to try and get Dad angry to find out what the secret was. I think it was a relief once it was out. They told me what little they knew — that my name was supposed to be the same as my birth mother's name and that she was supposed to be a nurse, but that was all they seemed to know and I didn't push for more. Mum said she felt very, very sorry for my birth mother and other birth mothers because they were being made to nurse and bathe and change their babies, and then they were taken off them.

'I was going steady with a boy at the time, and I don't know if it was a result of finding out I was adopted, but the next year I had a child and gave him up,' Gloria says matter-of-factly. 'It just coincided, just happened. It wasn't intentional but there might have been some connection. My adoptive mother was disappointed in me but I wasn't kicked out, they wanted me at home and I stayed there. Mum said that if she'd been well I could have kept the baby and she would have brought it up, but she was sick — she died just before I had the baby. I had support from the boyfriend. I'd gone out with him for four years but his parents wouldn't let us get married. We loved each other but I probably was a bit immature being so young— we were both only eighteen. He was an apprentice grocer and not earning much. Dad said we could have lived in their house, but it wasn't to be. It would've been a bit of a struggle, we might have come through, and sometimes the bigger the struggle you've got, the more you strive for. I didn't make the decision of adoption, it was just expected all round. There was no other option. I used to think if only there was a way, if somebody would mind it, but there was just never any offer, no suggestion, nothing. If there'd have been a choice I'd have been after it, but at the time I had no choice. It was always Social Welfare adoption, and I never got any counselling, no help at all from Welfare.'

Gloria gave birth to her first child, a son, in early 1964. He went to his adoptive home about two weeks after his birth. She never saw him, nor was she told anything about his new parents.

'I never wanted to give him up,' she says quietly, appearing reluctant to remember the emotions of the time. 'I always felt very sad about it. There was a lot of grief involved, but at the same time my adoptive mother had just died and it was all sort of there together. It was a terrible year but I came through it. I tried not to dwell on it, but it was the first contact I'd ever had with anybody who was related to me. I'd said I wouldn't look at him after the birth, and I didn't expect to be asked, but they did and I had to say no because I would've had a whole lot of new problems. I wouldn't have parted with him if I'd looked, I wouldn't have let go. In the first years I used to wonder about him a lot, especially every year on his birthday, not so much at Christmas. It was depressing but I wouldn't let it get to me. You carry so much around, though outwardly nobody knows.

'It was a couple of years later that I began to feel frustrated there was no way I could find out anything about my background. It was just a blank. I felt totally alone, though I knew that somewhere there might be brothers, sisters, parents I might look like — that was important, the physical looks, because I didn't look like anybody. I didn't do anything about it but if I'd seen a door opening anywhere I'd have been into that opening, trying to find something out. It was my birth mother I was interested in to start with because I felt you had to get to your birth mother to find out a bit about yourself and your background, and also possibly learn something about your birth father. She was the key.

'Then some years later, after I'd got married, had a family and adopted the children, I went to a group meeting for adoptive parents. I'd gone along with a girlfriend, to support her more than anything, but I was really more interested in a group for adoptees. It was there that I got the name of a man who knew all about searching for birth parents, and I went along to see him. My birth surname was quite common but he had contacts — a week later I had my mother's proper name! It wasn't quite the same as I'd been told by my parents; I'd been given her middle Christian name, and she had a different first name. So I went ahead and did a birth and marriage search and found out her age, her married name, where she lived and the address when she'd had me in Wellington. I went and had a look at that house and was sitting outside in my car looking at it and thinking . . . there was something there, almost a sadness. Then I got the name of a social worker in Christchurch, where my birth mother was now living, and he went round to see her . . . she just denied all knowledge of the adoption. He left a note in the letter box saying should she change her mind, or should she remember anything that could help, to contact him. Well she never did.

'I felt a little bit of frustration and anger, and I suppose hurt came into it, but I thought, I'm not giving up. I sat down straight away and wrote a big long letter to her just to reassure her on everything. I said that I didn't want to upset her or hurt her, that I wasn't a threat, that the rest of her family didn't need to know, that it could be just her secret and mine. I also told her a bit about myself, my home life, my husband and family, and that I was a birth mother too and could relate to it all. I never heard anything, and I didn't really expect to after she'd denied it all. But I had that stubborn streak in me that thought, she's not going to forget, I'm not going to let her. I started sending a small gift or a card to her on her birthday and at Christmas but there was never any recognition, even though my adoptive parents had said my mother never wanted to give me up. I was two or three weeks old when they got me, but she refused to sign the adoption papers for about eight months and there'd been quite a battle on about that. She actually signed them when she met her husband-to-be, but when they got married they found they couldn't have children.'

At the same time Gloria's thoughts were also very much on the son she had given up for adoption fifteen years earlier. She had no idea what his new name was or where he was living, and was only too aware that those facts were considered confidential. Through her involvement with adoption groups she discovered non-identifying background information was available from the Department of Social Welfare. Gloria was happy to hear her son had gone to a good home, but the department's superficial information was not enough.

'I was doing a lot of research then for people on the wrong side of the [adoption] law before the new law, the Adult Adoption

Information Act, came in,' she says. 'I'd worked out a system for tracing adoptees and I had quite a lot of luck. I knew that an adoptee's birth was usually registered within a few days, because I'd worked at Hutt Hospital and seen that when a single girl had a child there the birth registration was typed up and sent to the Registrar General's office straight away. So I'd look up the birth notices in the paper for the same time as the adoptee's birth and then look up some of the birth entries at the births, deaths and marriages registry office. I looked at them for about the same date my son was born and knew that I was within pages of his birth. Then I'd lift the bottom of the next page and write the name down and the next day I'd go back to the registry office and ask to look at that name. Each day I was getting another page over and eventually I found it! It had the original entry, the date of birth, place of birth, the name I gave him, my name and age, my address, and across it were the adoption details with his new name. You weren't allowed to see it, but in those days they weren't aware of what was going on and didn't try to cover it up.

'I found him and did a bit of spying! It was his fifteenth birthday and he was with his brother and sister. They were walking along the street and I was trying to work out which boy was the one — I picked the wrong one. It was shortly after that that I asked a social worker to contact his adoptive parents, but only for information. I didn't want contact because he was only fifteen and it'd be difficult for him at that age. The adoptive parents were anti, anti everything. They stirred up all sorts of trouble, went into Social Welfare and complained, blamed the department although they'd only done what I'd asked, said they were doing their best to bring him up and that I was interfering. They were very threatened. I didn't try to make contact again but I did manage to get a photo of him from school magazines, and I kept track of what he was doing.

'I also kept on sending things to my birth mother at Christmas and for her birthday. Then one year I wrote down to ask if she'd got the photos of my family that I'd sent about seven months prior. I got a letter back from her husband, with the photos, telling me to bugger off because I was disrupting their lives. I felt a bit frustrated, but it was from him, not her, plus the fact that these photos had been kept for seven months and not thrown out. I always had this little hope because my parents had said she'd wanted me, that sort of hung in there, and the photos had been held on to. So I thought, there's something there. I was so used to rejection — it wasn't getting me down — but I just kept reminding her that I existed.

'I did a bit of research into my birth mother's family to work out a family tree, and also to see if there was any dark blood, because I was always being told at school I must be part-Maori. But we can't trace any connections — everyone's been of English descent. I left it for a while and then decided to approach my grandmother, who was in her early seventies then and living in Hastings. I got a woman from the adoption support group there, Jenny, to go and visit her on my behalf, and she did a marvellous job. Jenny was there for four hours and had my grandmother crying. Apparently my grandmother had heard from some aunt that her daughter, my birth mother, had had a child and given it up, but my birth mother had never told her. At the same time my grandmother wanted to know how I'd found her, because my mother's birth was a secret. It's very confusing . . . my grandmother had been raped by her stepfather, and as a result my birth mother was born and handed over to her natural grandmother, my great-grandmother, and her husband, my step-great-grandfather, who was my birth mother's step-grandfather and in fact her birth father,' Gloria says slowly, trying to get the generations in the right place. 'My birth mother didn't have a happy childhood and she wasn't treated well — you can understand that. Her grandmother was quite good to her but at the same time she knew her husband, my birth mother's step-grandfather and birth father, had raped her daughter and she was bringing up the offspring. My grandmother said she wanted to know me but she felt very threatened. We've never met, because she's scared her other six children will find out that she had an older child who was raised by other members of the family.

'Through that visit I also found out that my birth mother's husband had died and she was now living alone, no children, no husband, totally alone. I thought, well he's out of the way now, but I waited about a year for her to get over that and then I got

Catholic Social Services to go and visit her. She told them to bugger off. I'd said that if she said no, then to ask about my birth father, but no, she wouldn't say anything about him. I felt a bit frustrated but I still kept thinking, I'm not giving up. I kept sending things at Christmas and on her birthday for the next two to three years, then one Christmas I thought, blow it, I'm not sending anything. Ten months later her birthday came round and I thought, will I, won't I? I left it too late to buy a card and send it, so after an adoption support group meeting I decided to send a red rose for her birthday. She fell apart when she got it, and then confided in a neighbour who's about my age. The neighbour was perming my mother's hair and the subject came up on the wireless. She'd always turned off the radio or television whenever anything came on about adoption, but this time she couldn't turn it off. They talked all weekend and it all came out. There must have been something there wanting and just waiting to be convinced, and the neighbour, Pat, did that and then rang me.

' "Hello . . . is that Gloria? It's Mrs Brown's neighbour, Pat, here. Did you send Mrs Brown a red rose?"

' "Yes," I said, thinking, oh God, what now?

' "Well, she wants to take it very slowly, you know, perhaps a few letters first . . . she'd like to get to know you."

'I couldn't believe it! It had taken seven years for that to happen — from complete denials to wanting to get to know me. I was used to coping the other way round and for it to suddenly spring around — I just went stupid! I was so excited I was jumping up and down! After I got off the phone I went rushing out looking for my husband, and he couldn't make sense of me.

'Pat told me such a lot and I got so confused. Over the next couple of days she'd go over and talk with my mother and then ring me up again to ask more questions. I had to pretend to be telling the gospel truth about how I'd found her, though I was lying through my teeth, because I had to protect the people who'd given me the name and address. I said my adoptive parents had told me her name, and it's true in a lot of cases, and just about true in mine. The neighbour also told me a lot of things over the phone — about my mother's upbringing, my grandmother's rape, my birth father — then swore me to secrecy.

'I had to write a letter to my mother, care of the neighbour, which I did, and then it was over to her. She wrote back and sent photos, and from then it was all on. She said she wanted to take her time and get to know me slowly, but within six weeks we met. She wrote and said, "Gloria, pack your bags, come and see me." I went down for four days, and gee, we were alike, and gee, we got on. It was mighty! I flew down by myself, I wanted to be totally alone, and I was pretty good until I got off the plane at Christchurch Airport. I was walking across the tarmac to the building and, as I approached those double doors with that sea of faces behind them, I thought, God, she'll be there looking for me, picking me out, but there'll just be a sea of faces and I won't know any. I walked in and looked to the right and here was this woman hiding behind the pillar, poking her head out, and next to her was a woman who fitted the description of the neighbour. I picked them out straight away and gave them all a hug and said, "How are you?" I kept full control.

'It was a bit nervy those first few hours. My mother was very nervous and had been dry-retching all morning, but everything worked out all right. We had a few drinks and talked that night, but not about the serious things — I thought that could wait because I had the four days. On the Saturday we went out shopping and got on like a house on fire. Then on the Sunday we sat there at home just having a few drinks — I don't usually drink all weekend! But it helped under those conditions and we really got talking. Her tongue loosened up and I heard all about my father.

'She was twenty-two when I was born in 1945, so I thought he might have been an American, it all fitted in round that time, but she said, "He's just a Kiwi." He played the drums in a band at the dance hall where she went on Saturday nights, and they'd been going out for a wee while when she got pregnant. But unbeknownst to her, and after she found out she was pregnant, she discovered he had a wife and two kids. She was at the dance one night, and sort of with him, when this woman came up to her and said, "What do you think you're doing? You're with my husband." They talked a few things out there and she found out that his wife was also just pregnant. She didn't want to have me adopted but there was no support in those days, nothing. She had no family with her and wasn't able to tell them because there was nobody she was close to. She was boarding with some people who took sympathy on her and looked after while she was pregnant. She stayed on afterwards and then they helped her get married from their place and were very good to her. She wasn't able to have more children and doesn't know why. Her husband was adopted, an in-family adoption, so there may have been something there.

'My mother said she didn't mind if I tried to find my father but she didn't want to know anything about it. I did quite a lot of research and even though he's got a common name, I found him in Rotorua. I was half-pie hoping in one sense that his marriage had broken up so I might have a better hope of contact, but he's still got the same wife. I got a social worker to contact him and while he was interested to hear he had another daughter and said he would sort of like to know me, he talked it over with his wife and she said no. So that's that for now. But he's got at least another eleven kids and I've traced most of them. I haven't contacted them but I like to know where they are. I actually got a photo of one brother, a half-brother, through a friend I helped to search for her birth mother and father. I was talking to her on the phone one day and said, "I've got a half-brother up your way. His name's Peter Stewart."

'He's a good family friend . . . I've got photos of him!' the friend said.

'Shh . . . don't say anything,' Gloria replied.

'I've also got a photo of another brother's eldest daughter, my niece,' Gloria adds. 'She was in the local rag in Whakatane and a friend cut it out and sent it to me. We're nothing alike. I'm more like my mother's side of the family, there's quite a strong resemblance there. All her side of the family have got the same dark skin and she always thought there was Maori blood there somewhere, but she said there's no dark blood. One of the first things she said the day we met was, "Lift up your skirt."

' "Why?" I said.

' "Show me your varicose veins."

' "I haven't got any!" She was so surprised because she has bad trouble with hers.

'We haven't really got any particular interests or anything in common, and I'm more outgoing than her, but we relate well. They say dirty minds can't be inherited — I inherited mine! It's terrible! But I've got an excuse now, and I've got to laugh at things like that. The girls at work can't get over the jokes she sends up to me! They say, "Yes, you've inherited that." '

Gloria and her birth mother have stayed in regular contact, writing to each other and visiting when they can. 'We met in the November,' she says, 'and then at Christmas my two eldest daughters went and stayed a week each with her. In March the family, the three youngest and my husband, and I went down to Picton for a few days' holiday and we talked her into coming up by train from Christchurch to meet the rest of the family. Then last Christmas she came up to Wellington for three weeks to stay with us. It was marvellous! We've tried to talk her into coming to live in Wellington but she says she doesn't want to live here, though she could still be on her own but have her family around to call on her. She's very stubborn, we both are, and very set in her ways, but she's got no excuse to stay down there, no ties.'

But while the relationship continues to strengthen, Gloria's birth mother refuses to discuss the seven years it took her to acknowledge her daughter. 'She denies having social workers around and tends to say she can't remember my letters,' Gloria says. 'I know to leave it alone. She could have wiped it from her mind, she could be embarrassed about it, but it's no big deal now. It's in the past and it doesn't matter.'

Since they met, New Zealand law has changed to allow adoptees and birth parents official access to identifying inform-ation about each other. Gloria hoped the changes, and the fact that the son she gave up for adoption was now an adult, might lead to contact with him. But the legislation includes provisions for both adoptees and birth parents to register a ten-year renewable veto to prevent identifying information about them being made available to the other party. Gloria's son has placed such a veto.

'I wasn't surprised about the veto,' she says, 'because he's had a good upbringing in a good family. No divorce or anything. He's had a good education and he's very close to his mother. That's good, it makes sense, and it's worth it to know that in his case I made the right decision. He's at varsity in Christchurch at the moment, and if he'd stayed with me I don't know if I could have got him there. He's not on the electoral rolls at all, so he can't be traced that way, but I've got contacts. I was also a postie for a number of years and he used to write to his mother — his address was on the back of the envelope! I don't know exactly where he is at the moment but I could find out. He knew I'd been inquiring, because his parents apparently told him, but I don't know exactly what he was told and what he wasn't. I'll wait. If it's another twenty years I don't care. Perhaps after his parents have passed on or something like that he'll want to know about his background. Maybe when he gets married — he's not married yet — surely a wife will want to know when they're having children?

'My eldest daughter would also like to meet her half-brother and I nearly jacked it up for them when she was going down to Christchurch to stay with my mother. Catholic Social Services could have contacted him and set up a meeting but I thought about my identity coming out . . . I was worried he might tell his parents and they wouldn't be happy and might come round or something. So I'll leave it for now. I think contact with him would also stir up a lot of old ghosts for his father. We met again a few years back and there are still some very strong feelings there, which we've got to ignore because we've both made new lives for ourselves now. You can't go back. But I've said to his father that I know where our son is and that.'

'I said, "If I have contact with him one day will you want to know?"

' 'Yes — though I haven't really thought about it," he said. "I also haven't told my wife . . ."

'But I reckon his wife knows,' Gloria says, 'because in Upper Hutt people knew everything if somebody had a child.'

Adoption is obviously very much part of Gloria's life. She is in the rare position of being able to look at adoption from each angle, each side of the personal triangle and through professional eyes. Strong opinions might be expected, but her tone when expressing views on the law and adoption policy is thoughtful and her words reflect the fact that no two cases are identical. She is strongly in favour of contact between adult adoptees and birth relatives, but says, 'At the same time I can understand vetoes but I think there should be something there in place of them, maybe some sort of counselling instead. I don't know how you get round it but I think they will be done away with eventually. It's very frightening for people, particularly birth parents, to think somebody might come knocking at their door or ringing them up and catching them unawares. And I can understand people placing a veto while they're searching, so they keep control of the situation. But anyone who does place a veto thinks they're safe, and they're not at all. There are so many ways of finding out.'

She supports the concept of open adoption from day one, but is also mindful of the human aspects involved, the individual considerations. 'I would have loved to have continuing contact with my son,' she says, 'but I don't know, I could've become impossible because I wanted to keep him. It would have been very hard to protect the child under those circumstances. It's different now. People are counselled and everything's talked out thoroughly. It might have worked out for us if it had all been talked out and I'd met the adoptive parents. I think all adoptions should be open now, as long as everything's talked out and the birth mother and adoptive parents want it that way. If not, adult adoptees can track down their birth parents.'

Gloria's personal experiences of being an adoptee and a birth mother have been heart-breaking at times but she has coped with the rejections and through her perseverance, which she now sees as inherited stubbornness, she has at least been rewarded with the tremendous joy of meeting her birth mother. Through all of this she is determined to see her adoptive children grow up in both a stable and an open environment.

'We didn't have contact with their birth mothers at the time,' she says, the regret obvious in her voice. 'It was never put to us, never mentioned. I could have got the names at the time but they weren't even on the documents we signed — they were left off and put in afterwards. We had to go back the hard way to trace their mothers. Trevor's mother got married and went to

Australia, but her marriage has broken up since. She's had an unhappy background, a terrible background, and I haven't told him any of that. He doesn't need to know it now — she can tell him one day. She was approached in Australia and told we wanted to make contact, but she said she wanted to straighten her life out. She was pleased for Trevor and said that if she came back to New Zealand she'd contact Barnardo's who'd then contact me. But I've had trouble tracing Jacqui's mother. She married a guy from Wales and they left the country to go travelling all around the place. I've since learnt that she's left him and she's been seen back in Christchurch, but I haven't found her. There's no divorce on her marriage, I checked that, and I've found no record of her in anything I've looked into. Actually Jacqui's also got an older brother who was put up for adoption. I was never told about that but I found out! It was in Christchurch, and I got Catholic Social Services to go and see his adoptive parents. We met them a couple of months back and they're a good Christian family. They met Jacqui but she hasn't met her brother yet — he's going through identity problems and he's out with street kids, running away and everything like that, but he's slowly settling down, particularly now he knows he's got a sister in Wellington. Jacqui knows about it, though I waited until I'd heard the outcome of the meeting with the parents before I told her anything, and she thinks it's great.

'Some people get on their high horse and say an adoptee hasn't got any rights and that once you're adopted you're it with the adoption family — I can't agree. If I was a Maori adopted by Pakehas, how could I be the same as them? You have got rights to know about your blood and genes, and if you want to know you should be allowed to.'

TEN

Moses in the bullrushes: Ian

Circumventing tight secrecy laws, Ian Hodge made contact with his birth mother three years before the Adult Adoption Information Bill was passed. He had been told he was adopted when he was about seven years old, and as an adult often thought about attempting to trace his birth mother. But it was only when he was forty and watching his own children growing up that he decided to turn his thoughts into action. Ian, a Wellington sales rep, is now a staunch believer in the rights of adoptees to information about their origins.

Ian clearly remembers the day he was told he was adopted. He was about seven years old, with an older brother and two younger sisters, when his adoptive parents decided it was time to tell him he was special for a different reason. The 'man to man' approach was chosen for their son, born during the Second World War.

'I was taken down the garden by my father and told the story about Moses and the bullrushes!' Ian laughs. 'Moses being the world's most famous adoptee, brought up by a princess, was how it was told to me, and how lucky I was to have been specially chosen. Reality tells me now that in most cases it was more to suit the parents' needs than the child's,' he adds. 'They adopted me, I subsequently found out, because Mum had lost a child through miscarriage and I was a replacement. She was told she could never have any more children — though she went on to have two more.' But at the time the Moses story didn't make much of an impact on Ian's young mind, apart from providing a sure method of taunting his brother with comments such as 'I know a secret you don't know', though it stayed with him and turned into questions as he grew older.

'We couldn't really talk about it openly at home, it wasn't a comfortable subject, but every now and again something would come up. The two mothers had actually met at the time, which was quite unusual, and at least my adoptive mother could give me a physical description, that was all, but it meant a lot. I was also told my birth father was American — that was one of the things that got me thinking, because America wasn't in the war when I was conceived and there certainly wouldn't have been any American troops here then.

'When I was a teenager I naively went and asked for my birth certificate, thinking that would tell me my natural parents' names,' he says. 'Of course it didn't. There was no specific reason for searching at that point, nothing I was consciously aware of, I just hoped to find out a bit about my background. People tell me now that you get these trigger points of teenage years, engagement, marriage, the birth of a child and that sort of thing. It started to become important to me again when I was in my thirties and could see my own children. I'd be sitting across the table looking at my daughter — she's got blue eyes, mine are green and my wife's are brown — and I'd think: where do things like that come from? Eventually I got cracking when I was about forty, before the new legislation.'

Ian broached the subject with his adoptive mother (his adoptive father had died several years earlier) and discovered she could remember his original surname. 'When it came to the point, my mother became quite helpful,' he says. 'She could see it was something I needed to know and even went to see their solicitor, who got a copy of my adoption certificate — which is quite ironic really, because some court registrars wouldn't give it out but the solicitor got a copy without any problems. It had my original name on it and through contacting the home where I was born I eventually managed to get hold of my birth mother's Christian names — which coincidentally are the same as my adoptive mother's. Then it was just a case of working through the electoral rolls and birth, death and marriage records. I can remember saying to my wife when I first saw my birth mother's name in an electoral roll that I felt for the first time that I had actually been born, because for an adoptee you're never really born, you just appear. I actually knew I had a mother.'

Ian discovered his birth mother, Roselie, was twenty-three at the time of his birth, married, but had registered him under her maiden name, which several years later she reverted to using. He was also surprised to find he had a full brother, just two years younger than him.

'I've never quite figured all this out, but from the records I assume her husband, who wasn't my father, was away in the war — and she must have got a bit lonely,' Ian smiles wryly, but accepting the circumstances of his birth without making any moral judgments. 'Then she went and did it again, but kept him, my full brother, and I think that was why she was divorced around that time. In some ways I wish I'd been kept too, but you can't do much about it, and in many ways I benefitted in being adopted.

'I felt I had quite a good idea of her background just through all the information from the electoral rolls, because I could see where she lived, what her and her husband's occupations were, and could form an idea of her socio-economic background. She moved around quite a bit and moved off the electoral rolls at one stage, so I thought, oh hell, she's died. But we tracked her down by doing marriage searches — she'd remarried, had a child and was widowed about a month after that, and then remarried again several years later — and eventually I found her current address in Auckland.'

Ian decided the best way to make contact with Roselie was through the Auckland-based adoption group Jigsaw. 'I'd been conditioned to think that someone else should make the contact,' he says, 'but having listened to other people, now I have my doubts that it was really necessary, and in some cases it's probably more an intrusion of privacy by putting a third party in between the two people concerned. But it was one of those things where you never really know and only hindsight can tell you whether you've done it the right way. Jigsaw contacted her and told me she was going to write to me, but a very long three weeks went by and I never heard from her. It was just before the May school holidays and I was going to take a couple of weeks off anyway, so we went up to Auckland and I said to Jigsaw, "I'm here, can you make contact again?" Which they did, and arranged for us to meet the next day.'

Nervous and excited, Ian arrived first at the arranged meeting spot in Auckland's colourful and busy Karangahape Road, and waited for the woman he hoped would at last be able to answer the questions that had gone around and around in his mind for so many years. 'Neither of us knew what each other looked like — she said afterwards she had hidden herself away and tried to figure out who it was, and if she didn't like the look of me she would walk away again!' he says. 'But that first meeting was disastrous — neither of us knew what to do and we hardly said a word. We went and had a cup of coffee, but I didn't like to pry too much, ask too many questions, and she wasn't very forthcoming. Her husband didn't know about me and it was complicated by the fact that he knew about my full brother, but she didn't dare front up and tell him she'd done it twice. And their marriage was just about on the rocks anyway — she's since left him. So we just talked about generalities really, but I remember coming back home and thinking just how beautiful she was. I told her a bit about myself and said I'd like her to meet my wife and children the next day — and it was from there that things really fell into place. She saw she had grandchildren she hadn't known about and met my wife, and she knew it was all real.

'It was important for me to be accepted and to get to know her, but I was really insecure and unsure about things. Initially she never admitted I had a full brother and just said she had two daughters, but when I went up again in the August school holidays I met him. I think he was just as nervous as I was! Neither of us said much, we didn't really have that much in common, and in many ways he's probably more like my adoptive brother than me. I also met my half-sisters but I was just introduced as a friend, the mother couldn't bring herself to tell them the truth, and it must have been a bit strange for them having this guy turn up who they'd never heard of before. I kept wishing my birth mother would tell them, because the rest of the family seemed to know who I was. One of my sisters, Cathy, looks very much like me, and my wife was quite sure she would have clicked. Eventually Cathy said to an aunty, "It must be a long-lost uncle or something who keeps popping up," and then the story came out.'

Ian has been accepted without question by his birth mother's family, and has a particularly good relationship with his half-sister, Cathy. But while his birth mother says she is pleased he made the contact, she is reluctant to become too close and refuses to talk in any depth about the past. Ian has never hugged her and would love to do so but is unsure how to initiate the physical closeness and what the reaction would be.

'We get on quite well,' he says, 'but she still clams up a bit if I pry too much for information. There are lots of things I would like to know, and if you get her in the right mood she'll come out with them, but I've also had to piece together quite a lot from what other relatives have said. Originally I thought I'd just be happy knowing about the background on my mother's side, that I wouldn't worry about my father, but as I've learnt about my mother, I really want to know about my father's side too. She's not keen on talking about it but has told me a fair bit. He died in his late fifties and I've managed to track down where he was buried. There's no American connection, I don't know where that came from, though I've heard of social workers telling people what they felt they wanted to hear, or even making the story up whether it was the truth or not. My birth mother's really cagey about the circumstances of the adoption, but apparently later on, when she was on her own, he used to go and visit her regularly and ask, "How's my boy [Ian's younger brother] getting on?" She used to go crook at him for saying that, but there was continuing contact and the rest of the family knew him, though I don't think they knew at that stage that he was our father. Also, I gather he wanted to marry her and she had the opportunity but never took it. He eventually married in about his mid-fifties, just after she remarried. I've got a few old photographs of him — I blew a couple up to see how he looked but they didn't come out too well. I would have liked to meet him, and I'm quite sure he would have been delighted to see me too.'

More than five years have passed since Ian stood in Karanga-hape Road waiting for Roselie, and mother and son still keep in touch by letter and see each other occasionally. Although their relationship is not close, Ian has never regretted making contact, and firmly believes the secrecy surrounding adoption is totally unnecessary.

'My wife says I've changed character a bit since I made contact,' he adds. 'I used to be shy and reserved, and it's certainly given me a lot more confidence. I'm a bit more extroverted than I used to be — I don't know why. It's probably just that confidence of knowing your identity . . . you feel you do belong to somebody.'

ELEVEN

Out of wedlock: Sister Theresa

Sister Theresa, a Roman Catholic nun for more than forty years, was adopted when a baby in the 1920s. In her fifties she suffered a nervous breakdown, and while her psychiatrist suggested knowledge of her birth origins might be helpful to her, she dismissed the thought. Ten years later the new Adult Adoption Information Act prompted her to follow up the suggestion. Although her birth mother is now dead, she successfully made contact with the surviving husband.

Kathleen was seven years old when one of her playmates blurted out a not-so-well-kept secret: 'You're adopted.' It was 1932 in a small New Zealand town.

'I was pretty upset but funnily enough I did believe it,' she says. 'Maybe my mother had told some of the neighbours at some stage, and you know how kids listen in on conversations, well I imagine they'd just picked it up somewhere and of course kept it till the time came when they let me have it. I went straight home and said to Mum, "Am I adopted?" '

'Yes you are,' Kathleen's adoptive mother replied. 'Who told you? What makes you think you are adopted?'

'Someone down the road told me,' the little girl said.

Her mother then added, 'You were born out of wedlock.'

'I didn't know what that was at that stage and looked it up in the dictionary, and from then on I had an inferiority complex,' she says.

But Kathleen now believes her problems stemmed not only from the sudden revelation that she was not her parents' natural daughter, but also from constant comparison with their natural daughter Elizabeth, who had died of meningitis when she was only twenty-one.

'I think about five years elapsed before they adopted me, but I never came up to what she was. I was always being told, "Elizabeth did this better than you did." I used to get this preached to me all the time. I was about six months old when I was adopted, but my parents, who are both dead now, were in their fifties and I always felt they were too old for me. They were very good to me but they were very strict, the old type of parents. I used to bring children home to play, but only twice would they ever let them stay. When I was older and wanted to have a party, Mum wouldn't let me because it would dirty the house — they were very house-proud people. I think they loved me as much as their own daughter. They said I was very much like her but I always had this put-down kind of feeling — though I don't think I was treated any differently than if I had been born to them.

'I felt very close to my mother but I was a bit scared of my father. Then of course as I grew older, knowing what illegitimacy meant and that it wasn't as acceptable as it is now, I felt I wasn't as good as anybody else and just got that into my head. When I went to school I felt as though I couldn't learn — although I had the ability. All the time I was at school I had the feeling I couldn't do things as well as anybody else — I think that's part of my being adopted.

'I can remember my adoptive mother saying once, "Your mother used to come and see you and used to go away crying because you wouldn't go to her, you used to cling to us." ' Kathleen cannot remember the young woman who would leave her home in tears.

'Then when I was nine or ten and a naughty nosy parker, one day I looked into the special box of papers my father used to keep in a room at home. I looked through all the papers and found this certificate — Mary Ruth Campbell — and I thought, this is me. I took it out and showed it to Dad and said, "This wouldn't be me, would it?" He was furious, but he said, "Yes it's you, it's yours." Nothing more was ever said, it was never mentioned again. I was a shy girl. I never asked them about sex or anything else and I grew up knowing almost nothing. In those days you didn't talk about it and I was too shy to ask. I think my parents would have reluctantly talked about adoption if I had asked, but they wouldn't have wanted to talk about it. When I look back now, I think that if I had known as much as I do now I would have loved to have talked about it — to let them know how I felt.'

Kathleen's illegitimacy not only made her feel personally uncomfortable, but also proved to be a stumbling block in her decision at twenty to become a Catholic nun.

'In those days convents didn't want to have anyone in their order who was illegitimate. I probably needed never to have mentioned it if I'd done it the right way. If I'd gone to a priest, maybe he could have got me into an order without mentioning it, but I thought my baptismal certificate has a different name and they might question it. I told them and the order said, "Oh no, it would be a slur on [their] order." That really made me feel bad. I was terribly upset about it. But I went to a priest later and told him and he said, "I'll fix it, I know someone who will take you."'

The order accepted Kathleen and she has been a nun, Sister Theresa, for more than forty years. She recently retired from teaching at a Catholic school. Seated in a tiny and immaculately tidy room at the convent, she is serene, her voice calm and quietly steady as she relates her story. She says that despite the problems of illegitimacy, she never thought a great deal about her birth origins and certainly never thought about trying to trace her birth mother or other relatives until the law was changed to allow adult adoptees access to records. However, the subject did come up when she had her nervous breakdown.

'I felt shocked when I learnt the meaning of "born out of wedlock" and felt as though I had some kind of a slur on me. I thought if she, my mother, had done something wrong like that, is it going to be something I'm going to inherit? I understand it now, but I worried over it and felt guilty about it, though it wasn't my guilt. All that came into the breakdown. I had to have the psychiatrist point out to me that I was labouring under a feeling of guilt that wasn't mine. The doctor said to me, "Do you think it would be any help if you got in contact with your real parents, because I think a lot of your trouble is your background." I said, "Oh no. I don't think that would be very helpful." It was only last year that I thought I'd give it a go. The change in law brought that on. I'd heard of the veto, but funnily enough it never entered my head, even if my mother was alive, that she would say no. I thought, I'm sure I'll get a good reception, something told me I would. I had no real picture of her in my mind, but I thought perhaps she would have been very young, seventeen or something, and hadn't been able to work and keep me.

'I never held anything against her either, even to this day. I think she did the best she could for me under the circumstances. I don't know exactly what prompted me last year to look for the family. I just thought I'd like to know if I had any relations, nieces or nephews or anything. I always felt a lone ranger, not having anyone [related by blood], and when the new law came in I thought, well I'll do something about it.'

Sister Theresa contacted the Social Welfare Department and had several interviews with an adoption social worker. While she already knew her birth names, a copy of her original birth certificate — now available through the new legislation — provided her birth mother's name and age, and with that she was able to obtain a copy of her birth mother's marriage certificate. Department records about her birth mother also unearthed a surprising amount of detailed information. They showed her birth mother, one of six brothers and sisters, was orphaned as a child when both parents died from influenza in the 1918 epidemic. They also showed that she had married a couple of years after Sister Theresa's birth and that her husband was aware of the child, though he was not the father.

Amongst the records was a statement made to a social worker by her birth mother, who was nineteen at the time.

My name is Constance Williams. I am presently employed at St Mary's Private Hospital as a general housekeeper. I first met Billy Stevens about two and a half years ago at Mr Cecil McPherson's place, where I was employed. He used to call at McPherson's every year. In March of last year, 1924, he again visited McPherson's and used to spend almost every Sunday evening there. I used to take part in conversation. Misconduct between us took place towards the end of April, and on the second and last occasion on the 7th of May 1924. Billy did not visit after the end of May, owing to me showing him a letter received by Miss Baxter [a social worker] to the effect that I was not to go out with anybody. I found out I was in trouble and later wrote to him about it. He did not reply but came to see me at Mrs Salsbury's, where I was employed. That would be the end of September. I told him I was in trouble and accused him of being the cause. He at first denied it and made a statement to the effect that it could have been anybody else. He then stated that if he had to marry me he would give me a dog's life of it. Before leaving he suggested misconduct but as I did not answer he went away. I then met him at the Show in November. I asked him what he intended doing and he replied, let the Government keep it. He told me not to tell anybody about it. No further conversation took place as my brother David came up just then. I have not seen him since that day. I have since written to him, but he has sent no reply. He is the only man who has ever had sexual intercourse with me. I swear he is the father of my child.

Sister Theresa makes few comments about her mother's words, except to say, 'It's just as well she didn't marry him, by the look of it.'

'Anyway, I had my mother's marriage certificate and the name was McCullock. It's not a common name and Sarah [the social worker] told me to look through the electoral rolls, though we had no idea what part of the country she was in. The Superior here said, "You're not going on your own, you are likely to be there for days, so I'll come with you and look through the rolls." We started off and she picked up the first directory and in five minutes she had it! I was absolutely thrilled to bits! We looked at the rolls further and found my mother's name was missing from 1981, so we thought she must have died. But I had my stepfather's name and address and Sarah said, "The next step now is that you've got to write a letter to him. Give it to me and I'll get in touch with the Welfare officer there and she'll take the letter to your stepfather and talk it over with him to see if he's agreeable to get in touch with you." I wrote to him and just told him that since the new regulation had come in, it had prompted me to make inquiries, and I guessed my mother had died and he was the nearest connection. I said that if it was possible I would like to have an interview with him, that I didn't want to rock the boat with his family and everything else and make things uncomfortable, and that I was eagerly awaiting his decision. The letter wasn't too difficult to write because I knew before I wrote that my mother had told him she had had a child, and it never entered my head that he would not accept me.'

Sister Theresa's intuition was right and her stepfather replied to the letter within a week. He wrote:

Dear Sister,
During the week an Adult Adoption lady called and after asking me a number of questions she handed me an envelope addressed to Frederick McCullock. I did not intend to open the envelope until she had gone but fortunately I did and enclosed was a three-page letter that had not been completed and was of course unsigned. She seemed surprised when I told her that a page was missing. After reading the letter I said I would write to you if I knew who it was from. She said she of course had known that the letter had come from you. Now to answer your questions about what took place prior to our marriage.

After being in one another's company for a good length of time, one day she told me that she had had a baby. I was, I suppose, rather taken aback and somewhat surprised. In our discussion she told me that the child, a girl, had been christened Mary and been adopted to people at Carterton and would be well looked after. She did not mention religion and I didn't think about that either, not that that would have made any difference to me. I have no doubt in my mind that she had arrived at a point in her life where she had met someone she liked, whom she could trust and rely on to keep her secret. She seemed sure that Mary had been accepted by these people, who would treat her as a member of the family and bring her up in the faith her mother wanted. We were both young and I suppose she did not feel we could do justice to the situation by keeping her when we eventually married.

After fifty-one years of life together we had not broken the promise, and in other words had not told a soul. As Constance has gone, you will have no worries from me in that direction, I would prefer it that way. I am enclosing a snap but unfor-

tunately it has been cut in half, but I will try and find a good
one some day when I go through the photos. Other photos
taken are with groups of people. When she dressed for a dance
she did look really delightful. What a pity the Lord has taken
people like that from us. You may rest assured that your mother
was a lovely woman and truly looked after me. I know that you
have spent a lot of time inquiring into records to enable you to
find me, so if you let me know what you would like further I will
try and relate little incidents that have taken place over the
years. It is strange your letter arrived on 20th May, just seven
years from the day she passed away.

   I will sign off now as this letter is just acknowledging receipt
of your inquiry.

Kind regards

Frederick McCullock

Sister Theresa was delighted with the response from her stepfather and, as she was travelling to a seminary in his area about
a month later, arranged to meet him.

'I wasn't nervous meeting him,' she says. 'I felt quite a warm-
ness towards him through his letters and I could tell that he was
well educated. When I met him he was a real gentleman. He
picked me up and hopped out of the car to open the door for me.
His shoes were shining and he was dressed beautifully. The home
was shining, even though he lived there on his own. We had
afternoon tea together and he took all the photos out and
showed me. He told me that his wife had told him about me
before they got married — they didn't have any wedding photos
because in those days if a person had a baby before she married
she wasn't a bride — so they were just married in a registry office.
He said, "She told me about you and I was a bit shocked at the
time — it's hard to believe that after all these years now you've
turned up."

'Their other children, three boys and a girl, didn't know anything about me but he said, "I've been thinking that it's more
acceptable in society now and I don't think they'd be troubled
by it, I think they'd accept it. I'm seriously thinking that between
now and the next time I see you of telling them and maybe you
can meet them at some stage."

'I'd like to meet them,' Sister Theresa says, 'but I wasn't pushing it, it was his idea. I can see the likeness in the boys, they're all fair, and the girl seems to take after her father. He also said, "Call me Fred . . . you know, you should have been a McCullock, we should have kept you, but we were both young and inexperienced and we didn't feel we could cope."

'I thought I'd find the meeting emotional, but I didn't. We visited the cemetery where my mother was buried and when we were going home he got out his hanky and started to cry. He said, "This is really very emotional for me . . . it's like meeting my wife again, you are so much like her. When she was dying, of cancer, she kept saying, 'Try and find out, try and find out . . .' She said it three times and they didn't know what she was talking about, but I did — that it was you she was referring to, try to find out about you. She didn't know you were a nun. And you know how people say they don't believe in mind communication — well at the time you said you were going through records I couldn't get you out of my mind."

'I was sad about my mother. I would love to have met her, but Fred said, "There's always a home for you here, you don't have to go anywhere when you come down here, you come and stay with me." He gave me a big hug and a kiss when I was going. He was really lovely.

'There were lots of things I could have asked him that I didn't think of at the time . . . there are so many things. The funny part of it was that he said, "You know when I got your letter, I wondered why you were wanting to meet me when you knew your mother was dead. I was quite nervous meeting you because I thought you wanted to give me the once-over to see whether I measured up to what you thought your mother should have married." I said, "How funny — that wasn't the case at all, you were the only contact. That's the only way I could have got any information about my mother." "I feel a lot better now you've told me that," he said.

'What I found was a little bit disappointing was that my mother was a Catholic and said that I was to be brought up in the Catholic faith, which I was. But my mother evidently left the Catholic Church and went to the Anglican Church because she was buried as an Anglican. Fred said that at the time he didn't question what religion she was; he said, "We're all Christian and it doesn't make much difference." But she still went to the Anglican Church.

'When I was leaving, he said, "Seeing as you were the first in the family and you missed out on a lot, I've got something in here I want you to have." I wouldn't have guessed in thirty years what it was. He said it was presented to him when he retired — it was the most gorgeous silver tray and silver teapot, hot-water jug, sugar basin. I brought it home and have got it here. It's beautiful.'

Sister Theresa has been keeping in touch with her stepfather and enjoying his long letters sent promptly in return to hers. She has no desire to find out more about her birth father and says, 'I wouldn't have anything to do with him. He sounds horrid, and I think he wouldn't want to know me either.

'I feel quite satisfied with as much as I know, but I would like to meet my half-brothers and sister if possible. I feel a lot more relaxed, a lot more happy now. I used to wonder, am I the child of any one of them — any one of my adoptive relations? It's a nice feeling to know I wasn't. It has changed my outlook, I couldn't tell you in what way, but I feel I've got a closer relationship or something now than I had before. It's more of a belonging feeling, even though my mother is dead.'

TWELVE

I just started sobbing: Ruth

Ruth grew up knowing she was adopted, and in her late twenties unsuccessfully attempted to find out her birth mother's name. But several years later, using the new Adult Adoption Information Act, she managed to trace her birth mother — only to discover she had recently died. However, Ruth now has a close friendship with her full sister, Sharon.

On a sunny afternoon in November, Ruth sat in her old white Mini, parked unobtrusively outside a Northland address, and wrote one of the most important letters in her life. She had always known she was adopted and at thirty-two had finally traced her birth mother to this address. But unsure of her birth mother's personal circumstances and who might open the mail, Ruth wrote what she hoped was a discreet letter which would lead to a meeting and the answers to many questions.

Dear Margaret,
My name is Ruth Anderson, though for a short while I was known as Catherine Young. I am thirty-two years old. And I am wondering if you would like to meet me? I very much want to meet you.

At present I live and work in Wellington, though I am soon going to move out to Lower Hutt, commuting in to my work, which involves shift work.

What more can I say? Except that I want to thank you very much. Even if you feel you don't want to meet me, I do want you to know this.

Some autobiographical details — I have grey eyes, high colouring, I enjoy music, have a degree in physics — these are all surface things. My parents are still living — they are in New

Plymouth, in the same house I grew up in. Dad is seventy-four
and Mother seventy-one today. I have no brothers and sisters,
and I am unmarried.

   I would so dearly like to talk to you. Is Andrew [Margaret's
husband] still living?

Love

Ruth

Ruth already knew a little about her birth mother, but it was
only with the Adult Adoption Information Act that she was able
to obtain enough information to get this far.

'I got my original birth certificate in early November and that
had my birth mother's full name on it,' she explains. 'I was going
to work that afternoon and had an hour to spare, so I went to
the public library and actually found her name in a 1954 electoral
roll — I couldn't find it anywhere else, but she existed, she had
actually existed! The next day I looked up the rolls again and still
couldn't find her name anywhere except in the 1954 one. I wasn't
quite sure what had happened, but I already knew she was older
and had come out to New Zealand from England to go nursing
here, so I thought she must have gone back to England. I
thought, bother it, but I'd do a marriage search anyway just in
case she'd got married here. I did the search — and there she was!
Her husband's name was Andrew Hamilton. I didn't know
whether he was my father because there wasn't any name on my
birth certificate. But the records showed his divorce and then
their marriage, and my grandparents' names. From that I just
went to the current electoral roll and found her name in the
Wellington Central roll, and his was there in the roll from three
years back, so I thought he might have died. I went straight from
there to Northland, where the address was, and sat in the car
and wrote the letter. I made it very general, so if anybody else
saw it they wouldn't realise what it was, and I gave phone
numbers and addresses so she could contact me anywhere! I
didn't have an envelope so I went to the supermarket and got
one and then shoved it in the letter-box.

'My parents had told me when I was three years old that I was
adopted,' she says. 'I didn't understand it then, but I've always

known. They are about forty years older than me because, my birth mother requested I go to older parents because she was thirty-seven, so my mother was thirty-eight and my father forty-two when I was adopted. I had no brothers or sisters and always regretted that because when you are a teenager you sort of want somebody on your side to deal with your parents. When I was eleven, Mum and Dad sat me down and told me all they knew, which was very little really. Dad only knew my mother's name was Young because he was looking across at the document when they were signing it, and he wasn't supposed to know that apparently. I didn't really think about it, but I did think, well my mother was an unmarried mother, this is a thing you don't really talk about. It was a bit of a shame thing — I felt that — it was not that my parents put it on me. I wondered about her, and then when I was older, in my twenties, I came to realise how difficult it would have been for her to give birth to a child and have it adopted. I really felt that pain of hers and from that point I really wanted to see her, talk to her, and say, "It's all right, I don't feel bitter towards you, let's be friends." I felt it was a real wrench for her.

'I joined Jigsaw but nothing happened through that. I later found out from a friend who was with Social Welfare that my first name was Catherine when I was born, and I was quite happy, I had an identity. You sort of wonder who you were before you were adopted. But I didn't realise the implication of the law as it was then — before the Adult Adoption Information Act — and when I found out my original name was Catherine Young I went straight to the Registrar General's office [for births, deaths and marriages] to see the birth certificate. But there was all sorts of umm-ing and aah-ing, and looking up this book and that book. Then they gave me this sheet of paper that said adoption records were confidential and if I wanted that changed I should write to my Member of Parliament, and I did that. I also tried to find out where I was born. According to my adoptive parents, I was born at Alexandra Home, but there are no records of anyone born there on that date. We checked Wellington Hospital too, but there was only one boy born on my birth date, so I'm still not really sure where I was born. But I knew my birth mother had been old, I knew that my father was getting a divorce but it hadn't come through, I knew my mother's surname but it was very common and you can't pin anybody down with a surname like Young, so it was only when the law changed that I could find out.

'When I wrote the letter I expected to be contacted pretty soon if I was going to be contacted at all, and so I waited, and waited, and waited. I think it was two days later . . . I came home from work late and my flatmate said, "Someone's been ringing for you, a Sharon Craig." But my birth mother's name was Margaret Hamilton, and Sharon Craig didn't mean a thing to me.'

Ruth's voice changes and her bright, enthusiastic manner softens as she remembers the conversation with Sharon that night.

'Ruth? I'm Sharon Craig, Craig is my married name, Hamilton is my maiden name . . . and I'm your sister, your full sister . . . you also have another full sister, Trisha, who's living in London at the moment . . . and you've got a niece, my daughter Katrina, she's four now. Mum told us about you . . . she married Dad, your father, about a year after you were born, when he got his divorce. I think I must be about four years younger than you, and Trisha must be about two years younger. Mum told us your new name was Ruth and somehow she'd found out the address where you were living when you were little. She went up to New Plymouth and went to see you, just to see how you were and that you were okay . . . you must have been about one or two.'

Ruth and Sharon talked about the family and then Ruth asked, 'When can I meet my mother, when can I meet her?'

'I'm sorry . . . Mum passed away about a month ago.'

Ruth was stunned.

'I kept on talking to her for a while,' she says, 'and we made a date to see each other. I was quite cool, calm and collected on the phone and then I cried the whole night. When I put the phone down I went and talked to my flatmate and another friend who was there. We were talking normally and I just started sobbing. I think the thing was that Sharon had told me about my mother coming to see me and I could never talk to her and say — there was so much I wanted to say to her — that it was okay, I'd had a good life, she shouldn't feel bad, that kind of thing. I also wanted to thank her for giving me life. My flatmate was really good, she just put her arm around my shoulder and let me cry. I eventually went to bed, but I'd go to sleep for a while and wake up and cry myself to sleep. In the morning I went to work, I had to be pretty calm and control when I could cry and when I couldn't — before, it had been uncontrollable. I rang my good friend Elizabeth and told her the chapter of my roots. I was telling her about my mother but that I'd got two sisters, and Elizabeth on the other end was crying too — she knew more about it than anybody else, she'd been so close to me. She said afterwards that I'd kept saying, "But I've got two sisters!"

'It helped having such good friends, they were with me, especially Elizabeth, she felt my sorrow and grief and joy. They are the sort of people that when I needed to cry they let me, they let me grieve. I needed to grieve and I got it done the way it should be done. I think Elizabeth Kubler-Ross, who's written about death and dying, says one of the worst things that causes grief is unfinished business — I've never read her book but this is a classic case. I never met my birth mother — in this death there was only unfinished business that should've been done, and now couldn't be done.

'It was a bit scary going to meet Sharon — my sister. I kept wondering, would she like me? Would she look at me and think, yuk! Would I like her? All these sorts of things were going round in my mind, but she's a really warm person, Sharon, just very warm and loving. She met me at the door and hugged me. We talked and talked and talked, and she showed me photos . . . it was wonderful because I'd never resembled anyone in my life before!'

It would be easy to mistake Ruth for her sister Trisha, or vice versa. The resemblance is astonishing. As children they were almost as much alike as identical twins, except for the two-year age difference, and even now they have similar haircuts and part their brown hair on the same side. The old black-and-white photographs of their mother show a woman who aged considerably from the time she met their father and then married him only a couple of years later. As Ruth says, it's not surprising her mother aged a great deal then; it must have been an incredibly difficult time for her. There is a slight physical resemblance between Ruth and her birth mother, but from the pictures of her parents together it is obvious she is their daughter. She jokes while looking closely at the photographs of her father — her distinctive nose is obviously his fault! The photographs of her mother are more closely studied, the face searched. There is joy and excitement in looking at the images she has now been able to hold in her hand for nearly a year. There is also a resigned sadness.

'I didn't yet know Sharon very well that day,' Ruth continues. 'We were looking at the photos and she was talking about something totally unrelated and suddenly I just burst into tears. She realised why and she just hugged me, it was really nice. I was very tense and when I get tense I get sinus, and I had a roaring headache, so our first meeting was quite short but we keep in touch. Sharon doesn't look very much like me, but it's funny, she said later somebody asked her what she thought when she met me and she said, "She's just the spitting image of my sister Trisha" — she recognised me immediately.

'Sharon was able to tell me all sorts of details I didn't know. Both she and Trisha knew I existed, and they knew the story about our mother coming to New Zealand. She came from England, was born in London and was the only child of her family. She came over here to do this nursing stint in New Zealand and met another expat, an Irishman. He was married at the time, his second marriage, and they got round together. I think it must have only been the next year that I was born. She was quite old when she had me — you know, the first man in her life. He was going to get a divorce but didn't hurry it up as he could've done, so she was a bit disappointed. She was going to have me adopted and then go back to England and start again. That would've been fine. But my father, after putting it off for a long while, apparently said, "Let's just get married anyway," so they got married as soon as the divorce came through. I was born in July, and the next June they were married, by which time I was adopted, of course, so they went on and had some more kids,' Ruth says, aware that the final adoption order, made six months after her birth, irrevocably sealed her legal status as her adoptive parents' daughter.

'Trisha and Sharon didn't have a very good childhood, because my father tended to be a violent man. It was the one marriage of my father's that lasted, but it was her doing, her keeping things together, apparently. I talked to somebody else who knew them and he said he had admiration for my mother, but all he could say about my father was that he was a bigoted Irishman. Apparently he just wasn't a very pleasant sort of a person. Sharon said he had been diagnosed as paranoid schizophrenic — that would explain why he was like that. She said when he was getting angry he'd shake and get really, really angry, and that he spent a lot of time alone. But she also said that she always knew he loved them, even when he was being unreasonable. He died two years before my mother. Sharon and Trisha both left home as soon as possible. Trisha went nursing up in Auckland, and they both went to England as soon as possible to get right away because they'd had so many negative experiences in their childhood. Trisha's now doing a degree course in engineering in London. I did a degree in physics myself, so it's interesting that Trisha, while she didn't have that opportunity as a child though she could have gone on at school, is doing that now. I think it's wonderful and have great admiration for her. Sharon got married in England and then came back to New Zealand and nursed our mother, who had cancer. That's really good, because our mother had thought she was all alone. Sharon's offered me some books that were her mother's — there's an interest in books all the way through the family, and my birth mother had heaps of books and spent a lot of time reading — but I said, no, not yet; if you're going to take them to the dump I'll have some, but I just don't feel right about coming in and getting things, even though Sharon's very willing to give me things.'

Ruth's childhood was stable, by comparison with her sisters', but in hindsight she sees differences between herself and her parents, which may have stemmed from the fact that she was adopted.

'My father's a carpenter and actually built the house we lived in and they still live in it. Mum and Dad are both quite quiet, my father reads a lot, but I found I could never really talk with them. It was either small talk or nothing at all. I didn't fit in right through, it's funny, isn't it? I like talking about things, sharing what I think, and that was never done in our house. My mother was apparently good at sports when she was young, but I've never been a sportswoman. She was also more a social person than me, and she always thought it was weird that I didn't go out much, and because I didn't do these "normal" sorts of things, she thought I was "abnormal". Then I realised I was just me, I was normal for the sort of person I was. Although I didn't fulfil my mother's expectations, I was still valid as a person. So I think the problem was that I was one type of person and my parents were another type. This happens in other families — I'm not sure whether it was because I was adopted. I was just different, and part of it was probably inherited. My mother was — I understand it better now — she was thirty-eight when she adopted me. She probably didn't feel confident bringing up a baby because of her age and never having had a baby before, so I think she always felt she had to be the perfect mother. She never really relaxed, never enjoyed it, never let things happen, and that made it difficult for me.

'I told Mum and Dad before the law changed that I wanted to trace my birth mother. My father was supportive but Mum was disgusted. She didn't want me to find out anything. It was, "You shouldn't be doing a thing like that." I think she felt threatened. My father, he's a feeling man, he just thought it was a very normal thing for me. He had tried to find out more about his own family because he knew his father had married for a second time and he had thought there might be children from the first marriage whom he didn't know about. He found out quite late in life that his father's first wife had died in childbirth and had never had any other children . . . so he understood about family things.

'I didn't tell them at first about finding my birth certificate because I knew what the reception would be. I knew my mother would be angry and my father would just be quietly supportive, but that would be it. I didn't want to rile them. Anyway, I wrote to them just after I'd met Sharon and I gave them the big story and then waited three weeks for a reply. I was worried about it, I thought, my goodness, what have they thought? Then I got a letter from my mother. I thought it would be from my father, but it was good that she wrote. It was a short letter. It said, "I didn't think you'd ever do this," and it was slightly bitter but trying to be accepting. She said, "It's good to know you'll have some family when we're gone." It was that sort of thing, reluctant. Mum also said it must have been a very traumatic experience for me, but to me it hadn't been traumatic. There was grief involved in not having met my birth mother, but it had been a good experience, very positive, it hadn't really thrown me for six. So I wrote back and said it was probably more traumatic for them than for me because I was finding out answers to questions and they were just beginning. I said I thought they'd probably realise in a few months that things hadn't really changed.

'A week or so later I went to visit them in New Plymouth. My father came to greet me and he hugged me and said, "Hello, Hamilton." I thought, Hamilton? Then, ah — my birth mother's name! It was a nice greeting, his acceptance of my roots, my past. I went in, and by this time my mother felt better about it and they were both interested in the photos. They were both really happy and I couldn't believe it — it was wonderful! My mother later came to see it as a wonderful "fairy story with a happy ending".

'It also brought things out in the open and for the very first time my adoptive mother shared her feelings. She had always been the perfect mother, never showing any weaknesses at all — although I could see them — and I felt I could at last relate to somebody who admitted they were weak in some way. I feel closer to them now. I think my parents, especially my mother, may have always wondered, "What will happen when she finds out?" And then I did find out and nothing happened, so it's no longer an issue for her. I think Mum worried about it and never faced it, and now that she doesn't worry it clears the air. It was pretty hard for them that I did it, but I think altogether they're happy now. My adoptive mother's sick at the moment. She's got cancer so she's not very mobile, but she said the other day, "When I get better you must bring Sharon and Katrina up to see me." She's not going to get better enough for that, but just the fact that she's said it is a really good thing. My having other family is positive for them as well as for me.

'Mum was also able to talk about the time when my birth mother had visited and how scared she had felt. I was about a year old and in a play-pen outside. My adoptive mother came outside and there was a woman near the front porch just looking at me. Mum said, "What do you want?" and my birth mother said, "It's okay, I'm just going." They didn't really talk at all — it was a strange sort of a meeting. Mum was scared silly that I would be stolen. She thought it was my birth mother because of the colouring — she had red cheeks and I had red cheeks even when I was a baby. She remembers, but because she was older and insecure, she told her sisters and her sisters tried to tell her it wasn't really my birth mother, that she was just imagining things. So Mum sort of put it to the back of her mind but never really forgot about it. It was something she'd never really faced till I told her again. It was a good thing for her to realise that it wasn't her imagination, even though she'd tried to make herself believe that.

'It really meant a lot to me that my birth mother wanted to see how I was. I was thrilled that she'd actually seen me, even if it was just for a few minutes. Sharon said, though she couldn't be sure, that she thought her mum had also joined Jigsaw, so it was strange that nothing happened. She also told me that our mother used to go to the library a lot, she loved reading, but she also used to look through the papers at exam time, so she saw that I'd got School Cert and U.E. and Bursary and a degree. She knew all those things, so I knew she really would have wanted to meet me, even though she never took the initiative of making contact. It was all incredibly sad that she died only about six weeks before . . .'

Ruth is quiet and reflective when speaking about the timing of her search and her birth mother's death. Her words are emotional but her tone is also one of acceptance. She cannot change the facts, and concentrates on the joy of finding her sisters. She also has a strong faith in God, which has played an important part in her grief and the healing process.

'I think I dealt with a lot of the feelings before I found out, and I did have quite a lot to work through. I felt rejected by my birth mother, although I knew it had been hard for her. I think babies feel that rejection when they are very young and removed from their mother for so many weeks until they are adopted, and it's something that stays with them. I felt I wasn't up to scratch as a human person, but that was really dealt with in the months before I found Sharon and Trisha. A friend counselled me and prayed with me. There were quite a lot of things from the past, and it was something I allowed God in to heal those things, although it was very difficult. To know that I have parents and see photos and the resemblance makes me feel less alone, but I felt whole before that. I didn't need that experience to make me feel whole because God had done it for me. It was great preparation for the meeting, because I didn't go into it feeling uneasy about myself, and I think if I had I would have been clingy towards them, towards Sharon, and tried to get them to fill a void in my life that I'd had until before then. Meeting Sharon, it hasn't been a big change for my inner self, but I think it's widened my horizons a bit, and it's really neat that I've got a family. I also feel a loyalty towards Sharon — that I'm there if she needs me. I feel like family with her, and she hasn't got any adult relations in New Zealand apart from me.'

Both Sharon and Trisha have met some of their father's relatives in Britain but did not feel drawn to them, and from their experiences Ruth feels no great desire to trace that side of the family. Their father apparently left home when he was only thirteen, joined the merchant navy a couple of years later, and cut all ties with his family. Their mother was an only child, so there are no close relatives of hers still living.

Contemplating all she has discovered, Ruth says, 'It was all good except that my birth mother had died — there was grief — but it wasn't a bad thing even to find that out. It was hard, but it wasn't hurtful. I'm still sad sometimes, but it couldn't be helped. It was a clean grief, there was no rejection about it. I know that she cared and that she thought of me quite a lot. I just wish I could have met her and returned her love, and in some way helped to heal the hurt of her losing a child.'

THIRTEEN

Vetoes

New Zealand's Adult Adoption Information Act is a major step forward in adoption legislation, but it does not give either adult adoptees or birth parents a total right to identifying information about each other. The Act includes a provision whereby both adoptees (nineteen years and older) and their birth parents can place a ten-year renewable veto to prevent the other party officially obtaining identifying information about them. However, it does not make it illegal to continue a search in spite of a veto, nor does it guarantee anonymity for those who desire it, just as the previous secrecy laws could not. And the fact that the legislation contains a veto provision means that some *adult* adoptees are still denied the right to full information about their origins.

The Act has to some extent catered for the future by specifying that vetoes cannot be placed by birth parents of adoptees born after 1 March 1986, and that those adoptees have the right to identifying information once they turn twenty — or to place a veto. However, this section is unlikely to have much relevance by the year 2006 because there are now very few adoptions to strangers, and in many cases the adoptive parents and birth parents at least meet, if not maintain some form of contact over the years.

The veto aspect of the 1985 law change was widely publicised, along with the other provisions of the Act, and from the date that vetoes could be placed (1 March 1986) until the legislation became fully active (1 September 1986), 653 vetoes were placed by adoptees, 1.3 per cent of the estimated total number of adult adoptees affected by the Act, and 2243 by birth parents. Taking into account that only thirty-five of those vetoes were placed by birth fathers (only a small number of birth fathers are named on original birth certificates and therefore are able to register a veto), a birth parent percentage is meaningless. The veto rate for birth mothers during that period is 4.42 per cent. (Figures are calculated on the estimate of about 50,000 adult adoptees affected by the Act.) By the end of 1987, a total of 980 adoptee vetoes and 2968 birth parent vetoes had been placed, with a small number removed. The number of vetoes placed each month had dropped to single figures, believed to be cases where the adoptee had just turned nineteen. A veto can be placed by telephone or letter once the adoptee is nineteen years of age or older, and the person placing it can also have it removed or renewed at any time during its ten-year life.

The number of vetoes clearly shows that some adoptees and a greater number of birth mothers are opposed to any form of contact with each other. But why? Social Welfare Department adoption staff and counsellors interviewed say that although the department welcomes either party to place a letter of explanation on their files for the other party, if they should inquire, there have been very few such letters placed. But from their impressions it appears:

> Some adoptees have placed vetoes because they feel they do not want contact at the present time but may do in the future — particularly for adoptees in their early twenties who are already facing many new things in their lives.
> Some have been influenced by their adoptive parents, who are, or the adoptee is under the belief that they are, fiercely opposed to contact.
> Some have a strong sense of having only one set of 'real' parents, their adoptive parents, and do not want to be contacted by their birth parents.

Some adoptees have also not placed vetoes because, under the legislation, they have a second right of veto if contacted by the department on behalf of a birth parent. (Under the Act, all birth parent-adoptee contacts must be made through a Department intermediary.)

Impressions of the birth mothers who have placed vetoes suggest the reasons are:

Some birth mothers have never told their present husband and/or their family about the adoption and are concerned about the reaction to an approach from the adoptee.

Some have shut off the painful experience of relinquishing a child and do not want to risk having to face it again.

Some feel it is not the right time for contact, particularly if they have teenage children, but may remove the veto in the future.

For some, placing a veto is their first opportunity to take control of, and have any power in, the adoption situation.

A small number have placed vetoes to prevent the adoptee contacting them out of the blue, but at the same time asking the department to make contact.

The following are some of the comments made by birth mothers who have placed vetoes (supplied by Social Welfare Department social workers):

'This is the hardest letter I have ever had to write.'

'I have never told anyone about the birth.'

'I have never told my husband or children and I cannot do it now after so many years.'

'It was not easy to agree to the adoption but there was no choice.'

'I had to do what my parents told me. I do not have an ill-feeling towards the child but I can't cope with the emotional effects of contact.'

'I have blocked out the memories of a traumatic and unhappy time and I would find it very painful to have to deal with them now.'

'Moral standards for solo parents have changed since I had my child.'

'I had no financial or moral support to keep my child.'

'Adoption was the only option open to me.'

'If I had had financial assistance I might have tried to keep my child in spite of opposition from the family.'

'If I ever feel less vulnerable I might consider lifting the veto.'

'I was very young and ignorant and I didn't know where to turn.'

'I can't take the chance of losing the respect of my husband and children.'

'I had to leave my home and live amongst strangers.'

'I still cannot cope with the feelings of shame and disgrace.'

'I was told to put it all behind me and I have done that so that now I don't want to bring it all up again.'

'I hope that he will respect the parents he has and think of them as his real parents.'

But being on the receiving end of a veto can be a devastating experience, particularly for adoptees, who, under the legislation, are sent news of the veto directly through the mail.

One adoptee, a middle-aged man, spoke of receiving the letter that told him his birth mother had placed a veto. 'It was one of the cruellest experiences I have ever been through . . . somehow, receiving the veto in the mail was absolutely devastating . . . I don't think people are quite aware of the devastation caused by a veto.'

A woman adoptee in her thirties said, 'I was just totally, totally shattered . . . I feel that as an adult we have a right to know our heritage.'

The following two interviews tell of the experience in more depth.

In his mid-twenties, Brian is married with a young family, and has always known he is adopted. Shortly after the Adult Adoption Information Act came into force he applied for a copy of his original birth certificate with the intention of tracing his birth mother. She had placed a veto.

He is a friendly and easy-going person, and was very much aware of how his approach might affect his birth mother and her family. He is still unsure how he would have made the approach, but it would have been with a great deal more sensitivity than the still-common myth that, given the freedom, adoptees will suddenly barge into their birth mothers' lives.

'You can't just walk up to the door and say, "Hi, I'm your son," he says. 'The thing is, have they told their husband and family? Do they want to know you? They gave you up twenty-five years ago, and that involves you to a certain degree, but you can't walk up twenty-five years later and say, "I'm your son" — that thought stops you in your tracks.

'It got closer and closer to the Act coming into law and I

applied for my birth certificate. Then I got this letter saying she had put a veto on — two weeks before the flaming law came in. The letter said the veto was in force for ten years unless I could prove my mother had died — how the hell can I prove she's died if I don't know who the hell she is?' Brian can laugh about it now, more than a year later, but he is obviously still distressed. The letter arrived when he was at work and his wife rang him about it. He asked her to open it and read it aloud over the phone. 'I cracked up . . . an hour later I went back to work,' he says. 'It had crossed my mind that there might be veto, but I didn't think it would happen. I was totally pissed off — but after a while I realised that she had done it for a reason, there must be a reason behind it, but I also thought, why the hell did she leave it so bloody late?

'I would have liked a reason for it; I know she must have had a good reason, maybe she's now married and has a family and it's not the time for me to come on the scene. But I know she's still out there and she's thinking, "How does it affect me and all of us?" And she felt at that particular point in time, leave it as it stands . . . she's still out there somewhere.'

Brian has considered continuing his search despite the veto, but decided against it. He puts it this way: 'I was talking to a friend who's a lawyer and he told me one devious way of how it can be done . . . but no, it's not fair. The veto — it's been done for a purpose and that's what it boils down to. Okay, I'm bitter that she's done it but I know it's been done for a reason . . . and I'm also pleased to a certain degree — the biggest thing is, how would it affect you? I don't know how I'd react to her if she walked in, I don't know how she'd react to me, and I don't know how it would affect my adoptive family, but I'm pretty sure they'd think I was trying to replace them — and I've got to think where would I be now if they hadn't adopted me.'

Brian's adoptive parents were fairly open about adoption when he was growing up, but he describes it as a 'non-subject'. His adoptive mother has said she is supportive of his search, but he feels her words do not represent her true feelings. 'To a certain degree I think she feels I'm trying to replace her,' he says. 'I've said, "No, I'm not trying to replace you, it's just trying to find out who I am, where I come from." I think she was both pleased and sorry about the veto.

'All I have about my [birth] family is a foolscap piece of paper supplied by the department [non-identifying information], and that really makes me hurt. But I also know I've got an adoptive family who really love me, and I can't replace them even if I do find out who my birth parents are.'

Born in New Zealand in 1951, Bernie Day grew up knowing he was adopted but under the false belief, fostered by his adoptive parents, that his natural mother had died during childbirth and his natural father shortly afterwards.

He had what he describes as an 'almost Vatican' Catholic upbringing, and has an elder brother, his adoptive parents' natural son, who is a priest. Bernie is now married with two children, and is a public relations executive for a large international company in Melbourne, Australia, where he has lived for the past seventeen years. He had a good relationship with his adoptive father, who died nearly fifteen years ago, but has had very little contact with his adoptive mother since he left home at seventeen. He clearly remembers his mother's words when at nineteen he visited the family for the first time in two years: 'What are you doing here? You can't stay here.' He stayed one night and did not see her again until he was thirty-five, when, prompted by his wife, who comes from a traditional Italian family, Bernie began trying to trace his origins. It was shortly before the Adult Adoption Information Bill was passed, and without enough information on which to base his search, he waited for the Bill to become law — only to discover a veto had been placed by his birth mother.

'Liz, my wife, wanted to find out whether there were any genetic defects on my side of the family that we needed to know about for our kids,' Bernie explains, 'and her curiosity started mildly to arouse mine. I say mildly, because I was never really that interested. We also weren't aware my birth mother was still alive — it never even entered my mind.'

Bernie, Liz and their two children visited New Zealand during the Christmas and New Year period of 1985/1986. It was his first visit home since 1971. 'One of the reasons we went was to see what we could do about finding out about my heritage — starting with my adoptive mother. But the first hurdle was to begin talking to her after all those many years of being apart; that was a major obstacle in itself. Once we collared that, then my objective was to get whatever information I could wring out of her, and then start sniffing around to see what else I could find.

'We met up with my adoptive mother at a motel in Nelson, where she was on holiday visiting my brother. Her first remarks upon opening the door were, "What the hell are you doing coming back after all these years?" I ignored the comment and politely said, "Hi!" I had Liz and the kids there, and we went in and spoke briefly — probably twenty-five minutes at the most. In that time she didn't say anything to the kids, only a few words to Liz, and seemed to grizzle a lot at me as if she just had this giant chip on her shoulder. We really didn't get very far, apart from making initial contact after so many years. I had expected a certain amount of cynicism, and I was dead right all the way.'

Bernie and family then went to visit his brother, a Catholic priest, whom he hadn't seen since 1969 but with whom he had been on friendly terms. However, the visit ended after only a five-minute conversation on the presbytery doorstep. 'He said he was going out and didn't have time to talk,' Bernie remembers. 'He was very, very cold . . . and he was really remarkably rude, I thought, for a priest.' Angry at the initial reception, Bernie decided against making a further visit, which had been arranged for the following day.

'But I thought I can't leave the country without at least seeing Mum again,' he says, and explains that he went to see her at her home in Auckland on the day the family was booked on a flight back to Australia. 'I had about a half-hour meeting with her. When I said to her, "I'm going to find out my real origins — what can you tell me?" she was rather taken aback and then said, "I'll help you in any way I can." So once she gathered her thoughts and agreed to that, she then opened up and told me where they got me from. Something didn't make sense and I said, "You always told me my mother died at birth." Mum quickly said, "That was what we were told to tell adoptees in the fifties." I got a little aggressive and suggested that wasn't quite the right approach even if it was in the fifties . . . here you are at thirty-five, thinking your mother died at birth, when in fact it was a whole load of cobblers. I was pissed off that I'd been spun all this bullshit for so long when there wasn't any need for it.

'I also asked Mum if she had any photos of me — she produced four or five and told me she'd burnt the rest. I felt rotten, in fact I felt really shithouse. Here you've got an adoptive mother who has picked up this kid on the way through life, supposedly to give it equal standing along with her own natural son, and then she decides halfway through life to chuck out all the memories.'

Following the only lead his adoptive mother has been willing to provide about his origins, and only about three hours before he was due to fly back to Melbourne, Bernie rang the Catholic hospital where he was born.

'Hello, my name is Bernie Day . . . I'm ringing because I'm adopted and interested in tracing my birth mother . . . my adoptive mother told me I was born at this hospital in 1951 . . .'

'I'll go and look up the records,' the elderly sister replied. A few minutes later she returned. 'Oh — it's very interesting — I remember this one . . .'

Bernie chatted to the sister for about an hour on the phone and learnt his birth mother's Christian name, where she was originally from, and that she was twenty-four when he was born and had been a milliner. The sister would not tell him the surname. There was no name on the records for his father.

'Had she given me a surname, I'd probably have postponed the trip home,' he says. 'But she was most helpful. I hadn't expected to get so much information in a phone call — it was a flying start! I think my birth was one of those unfortunate circumstances where this twenty-four-year-old lady got pregnant and couldn't get married to this fellow. She was sent up to Auckland so that she wouldn't be disgraced, but none of that worries me. What I can't understand is the bullshit that followed.'

When the Adult Adoption Information Act came into force Bernie applied for his original birth certificate in the hope it would provide the missing surname. His birth mother had placed a veto.

'I'm ratshit now for ten years,' he says, a little aggressively. 'What it told me was that my natural mother is certainly still alive and kicking, and that she sat down and considered her position.' He later adds, 'I'm a little disappointed considering the number of people who have been able to make contact in New Zealand. I'm saddened — I won't say I'm angry. I don't think I hold it so much against the natural mother, but more so against spin-offs of the system and the way the system operated in the sociological pressure that's brought to bear. If she's got a family of her own at the moment, maybe she thinks there would be too much pressure to bear from that quarter. It's very difficult to know. She might have a drunken bum of a husband and wouldn't want anyone on earth to bloody know what sort of torment she's gone through for the last thirty years. Maybe she ended up marrying the same father — you just don't know.'

After a lot of thought Bernie also says, 'I guess she has the right as an individual to remain silent, but I don't know whether she has the moral right to maintain silence against her own offspring. I guess I'm suggesting that it could be considered she has an obligation to me, that all natural mothers have a moral obligation to any offspring they've dumped in this world.

'Most of the curiosity is really Liz's, and it's been aroused in me. But I really don't worry about these things . . . I think it would be fantastic to meet her, to be honest, if it ever comes about. I wouldn't want to be meeting her to say, "Gee whizz, thirty-five years have gone past, let's pull it all together, let's start from scratch." But I think it would be fantastic to meet her, to get to know her, to be able to communicate with her as a friend, I guess. I also think it would be a terrific experience for the kids to meet with the person who is my natural mother — they've got an awful lot of negative things to say about my adoptive mother.

'I think adoptees have the right to knowledge of their origins, and without being bogged down with all the lies, deceit and bullshit that have been thrust down our throats by all these people who have been told to create the scenario in a distinctive way. I think adoptive parents have got to be able to take in tow the whole scenario of you having another side to your existence. While they might feel threatened, there shouldn't be any reason to. If you've been looked after by your adoptive parents there is no reason in the world to kick them in the guts and go the other way. The sociological framework back in those days set this thing up so there was total secrecy. Here you produced one baby who walked off with these people, and these people never met the natural parents of that baby. And frankly, I think the whole situation stinks. I think the whole system has got a hell of a lot to answer for for the fuck-up they created in the fifties.'

Some adoptees have continued their search in spite of a veto, obviously treading warily, and those who have been involved with resulting contacts say the majority are a positive experience for both parties — if the contact is handled sensitively.

The argument for the veto provisions within the Adult Adoption Information Act is that they will protect those who feel they cannot face the possibility of contact — and because it is retrospective legislation that opens the way for previous promises of confidentiality to be broken. However, all the people involved are *adults*, and 'normal' adults are not protected from the past by legislation. The veto option should be removed from the Act on the grounds of the human rights it denies some adoptees and birth parents. It could be replaced with provisions whereby both adult adoptees and birth parents can register a desire against contact, which must include a statement of explanation and, if requested, initial contact to be made only by the Social Welfare Department or an 'approved' counsellor/social worker. This would protect both parties from the possibility of an indiscreet or insensitive approach, but would not deny either adoptees or birth parents information to which they are morally entitled.

The Act, through the fact that it simply considers adoptees and birth parents, also in effect places a blanket veto on adoptees who wish to contact relatives other than their birth mother and father — such as brothers, sisters and grandparents — and vice versa.

An example of this is Grant's case, where the letter of the law, but not the spirit of it, has prevented two full brothers meeting.

Grant was relinquished for adoption in the early 1960s and, following the passing of the Act, successfully made contact with his birth mother and her family. He discovered that he had a full brother who had also been relinquished for adoption, but his birth mother did not know the adoptive name of her other son and unfortunately died a short time after Grant met her. Grant very much wanted to meet his brother but legally was not entitled to any identifying information about him. However, his hopes and those of other birth family members were raised when he discovered that his brother had traced their late birth mother and written to her husband, Jack, (not their father) seeking to make contact with the family. Grant was hopeful that, because his brother — who may not even be aware he has a brother who was also relinquished for adoption — had attempted to make contact with the family, the Social Welfare Department would assist the two brothers in contacting each other. The department staff member handling the case has refused.

FOURTEEN

Birth Parents

The birth mothers of today's adult adoptees are at the corner of the adoption 'triangle' that has probably suffered and lost the most through society's attitudes and the strict secrecy imposed in adoption practices until recent years. Many had no choice in the adoption decision. Prior to 1973 (when the Domestic Purposes Benefit for solo parents was introduced) many faced not only the stigma of being an 'unmarried mother', but also no conceivable means of supporting their child without financial assistance from either the father or their family. Many were young and naive when they became pregnant, and were an embarrassment to their families, who rushed them away to hide the growing pregnancy from friends and neighbours. Many were treated as second-class people, dirty and immoral, by some of the 'professionals' who were meant to be looking after their physical and emotional welfare. Some were denied even the opportunity to see their baby, and were made to swear they would never attempt to trace their daughter or son. They were told to put the experience of pregnancy and the birth of a live human being behind them; assured they would forget. But how can a woman just forget her child?

Some birth mothers have managed to block out, as much as the mind can, the fact that they relinquished a child for adoption and do not wish to be reminded of it. For example, a woman wrote to MP Jonathan Hunt in 1984 saying, 'I feel so very upset and out of my mind with worry. You see, I never told my husband that I had a child out of wedlock before I got married to him. When your news first came out [that he was attempting to change the law to allow adoptees and birth parents access to information about each other] I couldn't believe it at first because when I gave my child away I had to swear on the Bible that I would never try to find her . . . I really feel my life has ended and that there is no solution. I feel badly about giving my child away, I have done so always. But I really feel right now that I do not want her to find me.'

But for many birth mothers the experience — of giving away an 'unwanted' child and the fact that they have not even been allowed to know whether their child is alive and well — has had adverse and long-lasting effects. Some women have started to speak out, and in 1985 New Zealand's first birth mothers' organisation was formed. Based in Auckland, the Aotearoa Birthmothers' Support Group has become politically active in lobbying for changes in adoption legislation and procedures. At a grass-roots level it is a support group for women thinking about starting a search and making contact with the daughter or son they lost by adoption. The group states clearly the myths about the birth mother:

> She does not care about or want her baby.
> After relinquishment she forgets her child and gets on with her life.
> She doesn't want contact with or information about her daughter or son.
> The grief of relinquishment is the same as other grief situations.

The group also says:

> The effects of relinquishment — loss of a child by adoption — are negative and long-lasting.
> The loss remains constant even when contact is established with lost daughters or sons.
> There is an increasing sense of loss. The grief builds and does not diminish as in other grief reactions. The loss is worse on birthdays and other family occasions.
> The secrecy needed by society to cope with adoption imposes guilt, shame, worthlessness and loss of self-esteem on women, ultimately affecting their emotional, psychological, physical and spiritual health.
> The loss of the right to parent a first child affects parenting relationships with subsequent children.
> All relationships are ultimately affected adversely by the above negative effects of relinquishment.

Formal research in recent years also clearly shows the adverse effects of relinquishing a child for adoption (for example, Robin Winkler and Margaret van Keppel's 'Relinquishing Mothers in Adoption: their long-term adjustment', Institute of Family Studies, Melbourne, 1984). But instead of quoting from already published academic views, the words of the women themselves are the best illustration of those effects. The following paragraphs are edited extracts from some of the letters written to MP Jonathan Hunt supporting the (at that stage) proposed Adult Adoption Information Bill.

'. . . I adopted out a daughter fifteen years ago when I was a teenager. I have been bitter about the whole experience as I feel I was pressured into it, and not given any other choice. At the time I was not able to get hire purchase, or to go to a hotel, or even an A-rated movie, but I was convinced to sign away a human life . . . I would never want to upset my daughter or her parents, but I really think that if she ever wants to find me she should be able to. I would love to know her, and to be able to tell her that I gave her up because I loved her . . .'

'. . . Eleven years ago I placed a baby boy for adoption. I still believe my decision was the correct one, as I was very young and immature, as was my boyfriend, and we could not have coped . . . we married four years later and have subsequent children. We would never consider actively searching for our son although we think of him often. We would not like to upset him or the people who brought him up, but we think he should be able to find us, if and when the time comes that he wants to . . .'

'. . . I do not want to find my son to take him away or any such thing. All I want to do, and feel this is important for many and all, is to make sure he is all right . . .'

'. . . I am a birth mother of thirteen years ago, and far from "mental anguish" and "embarrassment", I would be delighted if my daughter was to look for me . . .'

'. . . I had a child adopted sixteen years ago . . . I have always wondered if he was all right and happy. Several of my friends who were in the same predicament as I was have all voiced their support [for the Adult Adoption Information Bill] and none feels a moral crisis — just a little sadness that they made a mistake when too young to know any better . . .'

'. . . I've never been one to go on crusades, but this I must put into writing . . . In 1963 I gave birth to a son, and because of circumstances I don't intend to go into, I had no choice but to have the child adopted. It is impossible to let you know the hurt and guilt that I've lived with all these past years . . .'

'. . . At the age of nineteen I gave birth to a beautiful son but, because of social pressures of the day, had the heartbreaking decision to make of having him adopted out. While doctors, relatives and kind friends all advised me to forget about this episode of my life and to start afresh, I was never able to forget this child nor abandon the guilt feelings that accompanied my decision . . .'

'. . . Eighteen years ago I gave up a baby for adoption and since then have spent much of that time agonising as to whether or not I did the right thing. You can imagine how I felt then when, a few months ago, it came to my notice that my daughter considered herself fortunate in, and happy with, her adoptive parents, and that she neither needed nor wanted anything from me. Part of me was relieved that she had had the kind of life I was promised she would at the time of the adoption, but another part was distressed that my suffering over this time had been so unnecessary . . . I can't stress enough how much having my questions answered has benefitted me. My depression and anxiety has gone. I have a new sense of direction in my life and feel relieved and strengthened, for it is the "not knowing" aspect of adoption that is the hardest to cope with — something people not personally involved find hard to imagine . . .'

And after the Bill was passed:

'. . . In 1967 my son — and only child — was relinquished for adoption, a decision forced on me by social pressures, financial circumstances, and total lack of family support. It was a decision I never made willingly, and I have grieved and fretted for nineteen years, fighting the administrative system and the religious organisations who coerced the adoption originally, for information and assistance regarding my son's welfare and progress. Now the Act is to be official I can hardly wait to confirm my research — I believe I know my son's name and whereabouts —

and live in hope of a reunion, when the boy wishes it so . . .'

'. . . I began to feel that for my peace of mind I needed to know what had happened to my son . . . to my utmost delight I was rung by the intermediary to say that my son and his parents had asked her to ring me and convey their warmest wishes — they were thrilled to receive my letter and wished to meet me as soon as possible. On their side they had apparently often wanted to contact me, so our eventual meeting was a very happy and joyful occasion . . . we now like to consider ourselves as an "extended family" and look forward to many years of life and love and sharing together. The experience of meeting me, from my son's position, has also been healthy and rewarding, giving him — as he told me — the part of himself he didn't know or understand, and helping to make him a whole person . . .'

The following pages are from face-to-face interviews with birth mothers.

At forty-six Barbara works as a secretary and is the 'respect-able' married woman with teenage children. Before she married she relinquished two daughters for adoption, the first in 1958, the second in 1964. In the past year she has met both daughters.

'I was sort of hustled off from a small town when I was four months pregnant [in 1958],' she says. 'You were totally scanda-lised into accepting it [adoption]. There was no DPB and no abortion. You had no money, and adoption was the only thing you did, there just weren't any other options. I didn't know much about the father, who was from out of town — he was engaged and she was pregnant and I felt I couldn't write to him, so he didn't know Carol existed. When she was born the only option I was offered was whether I wanted to care for her in hospital, and in lots of ways that was easier than not seeing her because she was very real for me.

'After that there was no way I was going to have any more children, nor was I going to have anything more to do with men, and I kept that promise. But about five years later . . . I was very lonely . . . and the next thing I was pregnant again after a party. There was no way I could have told my parents, so I worked as a "servant", looking after four children. When I had Jacqui I was totally anaesthetised and came to in a room with five other "naughty girls". I was kept there for ten days and signed the papers on the way out. When I asked to see her I was told if I looked I would have to take her. I wasn't even allowed to name her. After that I blocked it out completely and the only way I knew the date was to tie it in with a letter I got in hospital.

'The Pill had just come in then, but the doctor would only give any form of contraception to married women — it was the first bit of feminist feeling I had. Then it wasn't long after I left the hospital that I met my husband and got pregnant straight away and then got married . . . it was totally a replacement.'

Six years ago Carol's adoptive mother suddenly confronted Barbara at her workplace with the words: 'I'm your daughter's adoptive mother.'

'This woman just walked in and treated me like a piece of shit in the way she was talking to me,' Barbara recalls vividly. 'At one stage she said, "You bastard." She had followed me all my life — it felt like this great black widow spider. She approached me because she was worried about what her daughter was doing and thought it might help if we met. She set up a meeting in a public park . . . I sat there from 9.30 to 12.30 . . . when I got to work a note had been slipped under the door saying the adoptive mother decided it wasn't suitable. Her daughter was twenty-two at the time.'

Barbara planned to trace both her daughters when the Adult Adoption Information Act came into force — Carol found her first. But while both women wanted to meet, the reality of contact has not been easy.

'Carol was involved in drugs, prostitution and is a lesbian — and dumped all this on me on the first night. That didn't worry me, but it's just her whole attitude . . . I recognise where it's coming from . . . she was very bitter because she was adopted by much older parents and they couldn't cope with her.'

Barbara then attempted to make contact with Jacqui but was told by Social Welfare that Jacqui was only prepared to accept letters about medical information through the department. 'All I could do was cry,' she says. Barbara has since met her second daughter but only once. But through all of the difficulties she says, 'The knowing is important — it's the not knowing which is the worst of all. Contact . . . it's a healing process.

'The relationship I would like is just what I have with my other children — not seeing each other for weeks sometimes — gossipy phone calls — friends.'

Robyn, twenty-eight, relinquished her son Greg for adoption eleven years ago. Two years ago, at her request, the Social Welfare Department made contact with the adoptive parents, but while they were initially receptive to the idea of contact, they have become increasingly wary of allowing Robyn to meet her son and have not passed on to him any of her letters or photographs.

'I think I tried to block it [the adoption] out for many years and it's only been in the last four years that I've started to understand it,' she says, 'but I don't think I'll really be able to deal with it till I meet him. It's that whole "not knowing" thing . . . wanting to know he's alive and as I got older realising I had quite a lot to offer him — our family history is so much part of him. I've tried to reassure the adoptive parents that I'm not going to take Greg away and I only want to be a friend, but I think it is my right and his to know me. I really feel quite sad in some ways — it is their loss. In his teenage years I could be quite supportive, but I don't think they really connect with that. I think it boils down to adoptive parents' esteem-level over not being able to have children and when they do get children they become over-possessive. And I think one thing for me is that because I don't have any other children they feel very threatened.

'I believe you have given up your rights to parent but not to contact. Society says you have to give up all rights and it's for us [birth mothers] to claim them back for ourselves.'

Sonja, thirty-four, recently met the son she relinquished for adoption eighteen years ago.

'When I got pregnant it was something that shouldn't have happened but did one night . . . and then I really wasn't given a choice about the adoption,' she says. 'My mother said I had to go away because I was an embarrassment to my brother. I was sixteen. I was only three months pregnant but my mother just wanted me away . . . and said I couldn't come home with the baby. Nobody actually talked about my options.

'After the birth I asked to see him and they were a bit angry about that, and I only held him twice. I was told I had to get on with my life . . . but that was when things went wrong. My doctor put me on drugs — librium, valium — because I was depressed. I was addicted to the drugs for three to four years and then finally pulled myself out and coped with it. It didn't really go away but at least I learnt to survive. I felt better till I had my daughter [nine years later] and they looked so much alike as babies. I decided seven years ago to look for Andrew because I knew I couldn't get on with my life without finding him.'

The Social Welfare Department recently agreed to contact Andrew's adoptive parents on Sonja's behalf and they were happy for her to visit the family. As they lived in another city, Sonja stayed with the family for a weekend. Her face lights up when talking about her son.

'When I first saw him I just had a smile on my face and he had this constant grin for about a week — it was just amazing that I'd produced this tall, dark handsome hunk! I was really nervous but from the time I'd had a chat with his adoptive father first, we were all quite calm.

'I don't feel like a mother-figure, I feel like a friend and have been able to say, "My home is open to you, and my family all accept that." '

Sharon, forty, relinquished her daughter for adoption twenty-one years ago. She married less than a year later and had several more children in quick succession. Sharon and her daughter Christine met shortly after the Adult Adoption

Information Act came into force — both had been seeking each other — and now keep in regular contact.

'When I had Christine I thought I was in hospital for only a few days and I remember crying and crying — but I was actually in hospital for fourteen days . . . I was forced to wear a wedding ring and tell people I was married to a sailor who was overseas. Christine was adopted by a woman just after she had been widowed and her family thought a baby would help her — though she already had other children. I was aware she was going to a single parent and was happy about that because of my feminist beliefs. Some birth mothers feel that their child should go to a two-parent family, but when her father denied anything to do with it I thought to myself, "Fuck the bastards."

'One of the old myths is that you can forget, but you never do. It's a baby you carry inside you — you can't forget. I think I dealt with the grief by trying to be respectable and so I blocked it out. I didn't realise till years later that I spent twenty years quite depressed, and even now I still don't believe that I'm any good . . . there are times when I want to drink and drink and just block it all out. It was like a low-grade depression, like a grey blanket over me. Now I can lift it every so often and it's getting easier — I'm starting to feel stronger in myself.

'I needed to know the baby I lost was alive and well and cared for. I used to look at the death notices and think, is that my baby? Now I don't read them. I believe I relinquished the right to parent but not to contact — I firmly believe people who are blood-related have that right.'

Eileen, in her fifties, was married when she relinquished two of her sons, two and three, for adoption more than thirty years ago. At the time she felt she had no other option because of the circumstances of her marriage. A year ago she met one of her sons; the other has refused her request of contact.

'When I relinquished the boys I didn't grieve — I had to carry on with everything. They went away in May and that was always a sad time for me, and their birthdays. When the [Adult Adoption Information] Act came in I started thinking about it and wondered about the possibilities of contacting them, but I was frightened of what they might think of me. All along I wanted to make myself available — before the Act I thought about them but I didn't see how it was possible to meet them.

'I met one a year ago last Saturday. I used the Act . . . there were no vetoes and Social Welfare contacted both boys. One was willing to have contact by letter and the other said he would meet me — and then changed his mind. They were both married and had families. Alan [the one who agreed to contact by letter] rang me and ten minutes later I met him. He was the spitting image of his other brother I brought up . . . I now have another son and daughter-in-law and grandchildren and they're just like the others, they fit perfectly into the family.

'My other son . . . I wrote and never got a reply . . . but I understand his wife is adopted and has put a veto on . . . but even if I never meet him I know he's okay.

'It's made me feel perhaps a little bit more complete. I still have a lot of guilt feelings, and having found the boys has been good, but it has started a lot of things I've had to work through . . . it's made me think about the relationships with my other children — it really affects your life the whole way through.'

I was introduced to Colleen unexpectedly one lunch-time. Nearly two hours later I made my way out of the central city office block. I had read and heard the horrific stories of the trauma imposed on young, unmarried and pregnant women in the 1960s, but Colleen's graphic descriptions of her experience made them real. (She had also just met her son Pete, whom she had relinquished for adoption twenty-one years ago, a bare two weeks earlier.) She is an exuberant, warm and friendly woman in her late thirties. Unlike the other interviews used in this book, I took no notes while we spoke and my tape recorder was at home. But her story was firmly implanted in my mind . . .

Colleen and Barry were best friends from the time they were

both five years old. They were going to get married when they grew up, and nearly did. At eighteen Barry bought a house for them to live in, and the proposed marriage had the blessing of both their 'good Catholic' families. The young couple started having sex, but for Colleen, totally ignorant about the facts of life, it was simply a 'natural physical response' to their relationship. She didn't know they were 'sinning'. Several months later Colleen visited the family doctor because she wasn't feeling well and was often ill in the morning. Following the brutal — 'If you behave like a married woman, you'll be treated like one' — internal examination, the doctor informed her she was 'pregnant and due at the end of September'. Colleen had to look up the meaning of 'pregnant' in a dictionary because her mother had always used the term 'expecting'. She also wasn't aware that a woman grew large during pregnancy and stopped having periods.

Despite the planned marriage — which as far as Colleen and Barry were concerned was still on — both sets of parents turned against the relationship. Colleen's father's initial reaction was to attack her with his fists. He then put her on a plane out of town without telling her she was being sent to another district where she was to work for a farming family till the child was born and adopted. Despite being treated as a 'servant' by the family, she soon learned she was fortunate to be allowed to eat with them and made to visit the doctor regularly — other young pregnant women she met at the time were treated like 'slaves' by their employers, violently and sexually abused by the men around them and denied any form of pre-natal care.

Colleen went into labour knowing only that 'what goes in must come out', that childbirth was 'painful' and that in hospital 'you leave your pride at the door and pick it up again on the way out'. She remembers vividly her bewilderment and horror at what began happening to her — including the fact that when a nurse produced a razor to shave her pubic hair she believed it was to be used to slice open her pregnant stomach. On top of her gross ignorance, unmarried mothers were also treated as second-class patients; painkillers were out of the question for 'naughty girls', who should be made to suffer, milk accumulating painfully in her breasts was ignored, and seeing the child was strictly not permitted. Colleen hid in a broom cupboard each evening, waited until the coast was clear, and sneaked into the nursery to cuddle her son. Ten days after the birth she decided to keep him, but her baby had already been taken from the hospital and given to his adoptive parents. Despite the fact that she had not signed the consent papers, she was told it was too late to claim him back. Convinced by the authoritative figures around her that she had no choice, Colleen signed the adoption consent. The lawyer also told her she would be 'sent to prison' if she ever attempted to trace him.

Colleen had been writing to Barry throughout her pregnancy but he never replied. On returning home she told him she hated him and denied ever having had a child. Both married other people, and had more children, but neither forgot about their first-born. Eleven years after Pete's birth Colleen decided to trace him and that Barry should be aware of what she was doing. For the first time they were able to talk about the painful experience, and Colleen learnt that Barry had never received her letters — his mother had intercepted and destroyed them.

While Colleen managed to find out Pete's adoptive name and address, she went through ten years of facing hostility from some of the social workers she dealt with, and from his adoptive parents. But over that time his adoptive parents' attitudes eventually changed and Colleen and Pete, by this stage nineteen, began writing and then telephoning each other. Two weeks ago Pete and Colleen met. She is still glowing from the reunion, which also included her husband and their children, Barry's wife and children, and Pete's adoptive mother.

Colleen accepts that she is not Pete's 'Mum'; his adoptive mother fills that role. But she knows that her son is alive and well, and that he went to a home in which he was loved and well cared for. She expects to have ongoing contact with Pete, but at the same time believes she and Barry are more 'curiosity pieces in the jigsaw' and that his strongest ties will be formed with his half-brothers and sisters.

Towards the end of her story Colleen also spoke about the difficulties young single mothers faced in her time, when there was no Social Welfare benefit available, stiff social disapproval, and even if a woman managed to find employment and childcare she was paid less than a man. Without the qualifications or skills required to earn a good income the only way she could see of supporting her child was through prostitution. She considered it, but decided she was unable to do it, and relinquished her son for adoption. However, she is aware that many of the women she met when she had her child — and birth mothers she has met since — also considered this option; some went ahead with it.

'I remember asking a woman once how she had kept her child in those times,' Colleen added. 'She said, "The only way I knew how" — I knew what she meant.'

Colleen is not alone in her experiences. Her story of twenty-one years ago is shocking and appalling in today's social climate, her ignorance and treatment during pregnancy and birth almost unbelievable. But it happened, and happened to other birth mothers. Colleen was abused, deceived and lied to by the people she should have been able to trust.

The professionals tell us a great deal has changed in adoption practices over the past twenty years, and in New Zealand it certainly has. While the percentage of ex-nuptial births has increased, social attitudes have changed and the number of adoptions to strangers has dropped dramatically. Many of the birth mothers in this country now meet and virtually choose their children's adoptive parents, and ongoing contact, 'open adoption', is becoming increasingly common. But how long does it take for ingrained social attitudes, which can be either blatant or subtly displayed, to change? Twenty years is a very short period of time.

Birth fathers have the lowest profile in adoption, and yet it is most likely they were the instigators of the act leading to conception and later adoption. But while it is commonly assumed that the only role birth fathers play in adoption is that of a 'sperm bank', that their contribution to the adoptee is simply a pleasurable act of lust, the assumption is not always correct. Some adoptees do discover they are the result of a drunken one-night stand and that their birth father was either not told of their existence or denied paternity, but it is also far from uncommon for adoptees to discover they are the product of a long-term loving relationship, and in some cases that their birth parents later married each other.

The Adult Adoption Information Act allows birth fathers the same legal rights as birth mothers. (If the birth father's name does not appear on the original birth certificate, as is often the case, it can be retrospectively entered through legal proceedings, or more informal arrangements made if there appears to be no doubt over paternity.) But what of their moral and human rights over the question of contact with adult adoptees? It can be argued that birth fathers shirked their responsibilities to both the birth mother and their child purely by the fact that the adoption took place, and therefore should not have any right to seek out the adoptee in later years. They also did not have to go through pregnancy and childbirth. However, it can equally be claimed that human rights are, or at least should be, considered 'regardless of race, creed or sex', and therefore if a birth mother has the right to seek out and make contact with her daughter or son, so does a birth father.

In one of a small number of letters from birth fathers to MP Jonathan Hunt, one man, who supported the Adult Adoption Information Bill, wrote:

'. . . I lost a child to adoption when I was twenty in 1968 and although I expressed every wish to keep the child myself, I was — to put it mildly — running into brick walls at every turn. The mother of our child was seventeen at the time of birth, and considerable pressure was brought to bear upon her by her parents and by the people to whom she was sent to spend her last three months of pregnancy.

'. . . I would describe my own feelings during this period of my life as one of slow suffocation. Nowhere and not once through this has any compassion or feeling or consideration been shown for my point of view or desire for the child's future . . .'

Another birth father spoke of his views during an interview.

In 1966, Wayne, then eighteen, had sex with a girl he met at a party. They never met again but he was told by her friends that she was pregnant with his child, and that the baby girl was adopted shortly after birth. Rumour had it that the girl's father was furious and wanted to have the boy responsible charged because his daughter was only thirteen at the time. Wayne, aware that the girl did not know his full name, was too scared to contact her.

Twenty years later he says, 'I have always wanted to find out about my baby girl but been unable to. I have blocked out the details over the years and I have never been able to talk about it as I felt very ashamed . . . for so long I felt that I had no right to know, but now I have decided that I want to and will . . . but I find it hard to put into practice.

'The guilt has been the hardest to come to terms with, and I feel that only with contact with my birth daughter will I be able to resolve this.

'I've also come across quite a few birth fathers over the years — they don't usually talk about it — and whenever I've mentioned it, it's like dropping a clanger, it's not acceptable conversation. But generally the ones I have talked to have wondered a lot about what's happened to their child — whether they were in a relationship or not — but feel they don't have any right to contact. And there's the macho attitude of not admitting or showing any feelings and emotions.'

Does Wayne, and do other birth fathers, have a moral right to knowledge of their children? It is a question too easily answered by a hard-line 'no' on the grounds that if they didn't acknowledge paternity in the first place, they have no right to it today. The answer lies in the views of the many adoptees who believe they have a right to knowledge of their origins, both through contact with their birth mother *and* father, regardless of the circumstances surrounding their conception and birth.

FIFTEEN

Adoptive parents

A common cry heard from or on behalf of adoptive parents is that they are the forgotten corner of the adoption triangle. But in fact they are the only party which has actively sought to become part of the triangle, and therefore have always held the greatest amount of power within adoption. Secrecy has been in their favour, a way of pretending their children's birth parents never existed, and they have not needed to question that secrecy — until it was challenged. But the adoptee had no say in her or his place (obviously because of age), and while it can be said a birth mother chose to relinquish her child for adoption, many dispute the word 'chose'.

The strongest opposition to opening adoption records is usually heard from adoptive parents and those who claim to be speaking on their behalf. But why? Some of the letters to MP Jonathan Hunt opposing the Adult Adoption Information Bill go part of the way towards an explanation.

'. . . From my husband's and my point of view we adopted our daughter twenty-one years ago with the understanding that she was to be ours and ours alone, and we were assured that there was no way that there could be interference from her natural mother or father. Now we will all have to live with the uncertainty of our lives being disrupted . . .'

'. . . We believe that the Bill, although a sincere attempt to respond to the wishes of a minority of adopted persons in New Zealand, risks destroying the peace of mind and stable lives of many adopted children, their birth mothers and those lucky enough, like us, to be natural and adoptive parents . . .'

'. . . Our son is now nineteen and a half years and has a highly sensitive nature. Imagine the harm it could do him if having found his parents, he was once again rejected by them . . . we can assure you that should the natural parents present themselves at our door after twenty years, they would leave a great deal faster than they came, law or no law . . . they didn't want them twenty years ago, why upset a happy home out of curiosity now? . . .'

'. . . It seems to me that these sad mothers want the best of both worlds, to give up a baby when it is young, to avoid all responsibility for its keep, health, welfare, education, etc., then when it is old enough to work and assist them financially, they become desperate to contact the child and make sure by publishing long sad tales in the papers and magazines, so that the idea of contact is firmly established in the minds of any adopted children reading them . . .'

'. . . My husband, myself and our adopted daughter are angry that she has to write and put a veto on the possibility of her natural mother wanting information about her. Our daughter was most upset that she had to do this as she was very happy with the family that she has and she did not want to know, or to be worried by a woman she did not know, which could disrupt her whole life . . .'

'. . . Let us consider only the child. Of course they think about their origin and background; their birth parents and particularly why their mother did not keep them. They do wonder, "Why am I me?" . . . but we fail to see how our own young son or anyone will benefit if, when barely through adolescence, he is given the opportunity to identify and perhaps make contact with his birth parents. Imagine if the reality is nothing like the dream? Or if it is? Either way, such a revelation could render a scarring blow on a young person and could even cast him or her as a pawn between a birth mother who has lingering regrets over her decision of yesteryear and adoptive parents who know only to love and cherish the child in the same way they do, or would, their own birth children . . .'

The letters show a great deal of misunderstanding about the feelings of both adoptees and birth parents. It is commendable that many adoptive parents care so deeply for their children that they wish to save them from possibly painful and traumatic experiences. However, in the context of the Adult Adoption Information Act, and this book, the subject is not adopted *children*. Adoptees, as with all adults, face difficulties from time to time throughout their lives. Parents do not own their children, and must allow them to mature, to eventually make their own decisions and lead their own lives without constant protection from the unknown. In discouraging or preventing, either overtly or subtly, adoptees from tracing their origins, adoptive parents may in fact be denying their daughters and sons great joy and peace of mind.

Many adoptees speak about their adoptive parents feeling 'threatened' by the prospect of contact with birth relatives (though in some cases the feelings may be perceived rather than real), and some search in secret, in the hope of protecting their parents from the emotions of pain and rejection. But what are adoptive parents threatened by? Their own infertility and insecurities because their children were not born to them? A belief or fear that their daughters or sons will desert them in favour of a stranger or group of strangers, albeit related by blood? An adoptee's relationship with her or his birth mother, father, sister or grandparent can be very special, but how can it possibly replace the bond and emotional ties with the family she or he grew up with? Adoptees often have a fierce loyalty towards their adoptive parents, and if the relationships are built on love and caring, contact with birth relatives will often strengthen the bonds.

But not all adoptive parents are opposed to their daughters and sons meeting their birth relatives. Some are wonderfully supportive and understanding of the situation, as the following letters show.

'. . . However carefully they have been placed and well loved, adopted people I have known often feel the "odd one out" and the "void" area of their lives tends to dominate their thinking. I don't want this for my son . . .'

'. . . No one is following the [Adult Adoption Information] Bill more closely than our twelve-year-old daughter, who is an adopted child. When she was seven years old, we were chatting about her adoption, at her request, and she was asking questions about her natural mother that we were unable to answer. She thought for a few moments and then said, "I wish I could see her face." Why should our daughter have a lifetime of wishing, and perhaps fears and fantasies about her origins? . . .'

'. . . As Pakeha parents we have an adopted Maori son, age sixteen. He suffered racial taunts at school . . . it is very necessary for him to know his whakapapa for his racial identity . . .'

And an adoptive father whose daughter used the Adult Adoption Information Act to trace her birth mother and has since formed a close relationship with her now says, 'It's opened up our hearts, opened up our feelings about adoption . . . we were apprehensive and probably a little anti the Bill, but in hindsight we were wrong.'

MP Fran Wilde, sponsor of the Adult Adoption Information Bill when it was passed, and herself an adoptive mother, puts it this way:

'When we adopted our first child in 1971 the prevailing idea was that the adoption was total and anonymous, and that was best. You never told these kids who they were — you didn't even know — and they became integrated into your family. That's what we were told and Social Welfare was quite strong about it . . . this was the philosophy, the best thing for the child. I'd never thought about all this — we just wanted children and we weren't having our own, so I went in open-minded, just listening to the department. But it wasn't long after we had the child that of course I began to think about it a bit more — once the child was physically present it's pretty hard not to think about these things and we started to get to know a lot of other adoptive parents and started an adoption support group. It was initially all adoptive parents (later growing to include adoptees and birth parents) who were pretty well coming to the view that more openness in adoption was a good idea. But there were other issues for us as well — just learning to cope with being an adoptive parent, which is different from being a birth parent. We then adopted two more children in succession, and by the time we got to the last one I was totally committed to knowing who they were and them knowing who they were.'

Perhaps the most significant question in looking at the views of adoptive parents is why do people choose to have children? In the age of a rapidly growing world population despite reliable contraception, the (Western) social attitude that it is selfish not to have children — plural — still prevails. High-tech infertility clinics are doing a roaring trade; infertility support groups are springing up and gaining a high public profile; some childless couples are spending thousands of dollars to import Third World babies into their homes because the local supply of babies available for adoption has virtually dried up. In fact the driving force behind the decision (for those who are fortunate enough to have the choice) to have — or adopt — a child is primarily to fulfil their own needs and desires to be parents, rather than purely for the benefit of the child. It is not wrong or unnatural to desire children — it is human nature; 'survival of the species' — but adoption should not be dressed up in terms of simply providing 'unwanted babies' for people who are kind and generous enough to welcome an unknown child into their home. It should be defined in terms of providing the best possible environment for the child whose natural parents, for whatever reason, are unable to do so. And it must also be remembered that no person, no matter what age or legal status, can be owned by another.

The following paragraph is an extract from a letter by a woman who is both a birth mother and an adoptive mother, written to Jonathan Hunt in 1982. It shows great understanding of the issues involved.

'Those of us who are adoptive parents may need to show some of the same generosity which prompted the mothers of our children to give them to us originally. Children are not possessions to be disposed of as we will, but people in their own right. Adoption is, hopefully, about happy children growing into secure adults with the same right to have their questions answered as the rest of us. They should not be required to remain chained to their "owners", as it were, by a mixture of guilt and fear. Moreover, from my own experience, a contact with the birth parent generally only increases the bond in the adoptive family. The years of childhood are when the loving links are forged, and these, far from falling apart, tend to become even stronger once the adopted person's curiosity is laid to rest and he learns the truth about himself.'

SIXTEEN

Adoption Today

The secrecy surrounding adoption and subsequent debate over fully opening records should have little relevance by the time the children adopted in New Zealand today have become adults. The number of adoptions to strangers in this country has dropped steadily since the peak of 2617 in 1968 (75.3 per cent of all adoptions that year) to only 322 in 1986 (31 per cent), and adoption practices have changed significantly in those years with some now being 'open'. However, as society becomes more sophisticated, new questions and issues arise.

Open adoption

In the mid-1970s some New Zealand Social Welfare Department social workers began offering adoptive and birth parents the option of an 'open adoption' in place of the closed and secretive practices of earlier years. In its truest form, open adoption means that the birth and adoptive parents meet and exchange identifying information about each other prior to the adoption consent being signed, and that the birth parent or parents relinquish legal and basic child-rearing rights to the adoptive parents but retain the right to continuing contact with their daughter or son. In this way the adoptee grows up knowing her or his birth relatives and the true relationships that exist between the families. However, various degrees of openness have developed from the basic concept and the term now encompasses a wide variety of situations, such as the occasional exchange of letters and photographs through a third party, or the adoptee growing up knowing her or his birth mother but only as a friend of the family rather than in the context of the true relationship.

By the mid-1980s the Social Welfare Department was offering birth mothers the final choice of adoptive parents from profiles of two or three 'approved' couples, and many birth mothers at least met the prospective adoptive parents of their children prior to signing the adoption consent. In some cases contact continues on a regular basis, with the adoptees aware that 'Mum' and 'Dad' are their adoptive parents and 'Janet' and 'John' are their birth parents. However, open adoption in its fullest sense is not co-parenting; the adoptive parents are the 'psychological' parents.

Social Welfare Department Assistant Director of Adoption and Foster Care from 1978 to 1987, Ann Corcoran, says a 1985–1987 study found clear evidence that birth mothers who had met with the adoptive parents or had access to contact of some kind were happy about it and felt it helped them accept adoption for their child. There was also no evidence to suggest that the child was disadvantaged by contact; indeed, most adoptive parents who had met with the birth parents believed the experience had been positively beneficial to the relationship.

'Our experience, now supported by research, is that information carefully given is never harmful, and that meetings between birth parents and adoptive parents, carefully prepared for, are positively beneficial to both parties,' she says. 'While it is too early yet to speak for the adopted adult, what we do know is that the past social work practices of secrecy are damaging and destructive to many adoptees who continue to search for that missing part of themselves.'

A 1987 study of open adoption placements, by then Social Welfare Department social worker Mary Iwanek, also found that open adoption can be a positive experience and helpful to both birth and adoptive parents. (Although the study sample was small and not random, the same criticisms can be applied to much of the professional research into adoption generally, both in New Zealand and overseas.)

Mary Iwanek says the study revealed: 'All [the] birth mothers found the experiences of open adoption positive and relieved the stress they felt at the time of relinquishment and subsequently. All [the] adoptive parents supported open adoption and felt it had not interfered with the bonding process and feelings of entitlement to the child, in fact many felt it had enhanced it.' She also says: 'The study showed that those contemplating open adoption are regarded as deviating from the norms of society and strong pressures are brought to bear on all concerned to conform. Open adoption is a subject that reveals deeply held but rarely expressed values about the nature of parenthood, parental rights, ownership of children and sexual morality.

'The findings of this study suggest that adoption practices should be considered in the light of other changing phenomena in society. Many of the problems faced by adoptive families have much in common with patterns evolving in so-called "ordinary" families, who experience divorce and remarriage, creating numerous step-parent households. These families deal with complex and overlapping loyalties, which demand a special emphasis on acceptance of differences, good communication and trust — all these needs are similar to those we are attempting to deal with in adoption.

'Open adoption is neither easy nor problem-free. There is no way people can be guaranteed total protection in their lives, as all living involves risk-taking. It seems from the research that there is less risk of "losing" the child in an open adoption based on honesty than there is in the traditional secret adoption.'

Open adoption is perfectly legal within New Zealand's traditional adoption legislation, but although allowing for individuals to make any arrangements they wish to, it cannot be enforced and either party can refuse to continue the arrangements at any time.

New Zealand's Adoption Act 1955 was under review at the time of writing.

Inter-country Adoption

The rapidly decreasing number of 'healthy, white' babies available for adoption, both in New Zealand and other comparable countries, has meant prospective adopters have begun to extend their horizons in search of a child. Some infertile couples unable to get to 'the top of the adoption list', and in some cases not even allowed on the 'list' for a variety of reasons, have turned to importing children from Third World countries.

While the practice is not common in New Zealand, it is familiar in some parts of the world, particularly the Scandanavian countries and to a lesser extent France and Holland, which are importing hundreds of children from less advantaged countries such as India, the Philippines and South America. Inter-country adoption is often seen as fashionable, proof of non-racist attitudes, and saving children from poverty and possible death. However, there are other issues involved underneath the superficial image of the apparent generosity of people prepared to spend sometimes tens of thousands of dollars to obtain children from such countries — officially or through black markets. The issues of ownership of children, the rights of the adoptee to her or his own cultural identity, and the rights of the natural parents must be examined prior to any consideration of the needs of childless couples.

New Zealand's Social Welfare Department's general policy is that children should be adopted into families of their own ethnic and cultural group, not because different ethnic groups make better parents, but because a family that mirrors the child's own cultural background will provide the most compatible environment. Inter-country adoption is not consistent with that policy, and the department does not encourage or provide any form of overseas adoption service, apart from making the occasional home study when requested by an overseas agency on behalf of a couple who have initiated an inter-country adoption. Social workers also stress that all adoptions should be seen in terms of finding the best possible homes for children whose natural parents are unable to care for them, rather than finding children for childless couples.

Ann Corcoran says there is growing concern over the number of children being passed around countries, and the international situation presented both formally and informally at the 1987 International Adoption Conference in Athens, Greece, portrayed a very disturbing picture. In some cases adoptive parents knew little more about their child than her or his country of origin.

'While research does show that these foreign children do very well in the country of their adoption,' she says, 'it also shows quite clearly that they are raised as children of that country and that there is little if any notice paid to their sense of self, their own identity, and the rights they have to know who they are.

'There is little doubt that a tremendous amount of money is being exchanged so that children can be moved from one country to the other, and I believe as more pressure is placed upon infertile couples because of the sharp decrease in the number of local children needing adoptive homes found for them, a great deal of emotional and political pressure will be put on this agency to subscribe to inter-country adoptions.'

The conference passed a statement, forwarded to the Secretary General of the United Nations, which included the following paragraph:

'We are deeply concerned about certain still-prevailing attitudes which either ignore or diminish the "best interests" of the child in adoption services. The child should never be allowed to become a mere "commodity" in either domestic or inter-country adoptions for couples or other persons wishing to adopt, or for unscrupulous, sometimes profit-making, placement agents.'

While inter-country adoption is still rare in New Zealand, the Social Welfare Department is aware of a handful of 'very questionable' adoptions of South American children where New Zealand couples have travelled overseas, adopted and returned home with the child. In most cases an overseas adoption is recognised by New Zealand law, depending in which country the adoption order was made. If it is not recognised, the child's status becomes an Immigration Department matter, and can result in a complex moral dilemma, particularly if the couple are not considered 'suitable' adoptive parents by the Social Welfare Department.

In 1987 the British Agencies for Adoption and Fostering (BAAF) produced a policy statement reflecting their concern over the short-term problems and long-term effects of inter-country adoption (*Daily Telegraph*, July 1987). This stressed a belief that it is in the best interests of the children to grow up within their families of origin, not least because trans-racial placements militate against children developing a positive racial identity and demand an ability to cope with being black in our inherently racist society. It also pointed out that because services in some countries may be poorly developed, parents releasing their children for inter-country adoption are denied realistic freedom of choice.

BAAF believes that inter-country adoption should only be considered when the child has been orphaned, abandoned or its parents have freely requested adoption and are fully aware of the implications; where no one suitable within the extended family or local community can be found to care for the child; or where adoption or long-term care are not possible in the country of origin.

If prospective inter-country adoptive parents really have the best interests of 'unwanted' or 'abandoned' children at heart, the thousands upon thousands of dollars they spend in virtually 'buying' children to grace their own homes would have far more value and help a far greater number of children if it were put to use in preventing the circumstances in which children are relinquished for adoption.

New birth technologies

Medical technology used to assist women unable to conceive naturally may, on the surface, appear to have little relevance to adoption. However, some of the same issues are involved when the children created are not blood-related to either or both of their 'parents'.

While artificial insemination by donor (AID) is by no means a new practice, sperm can now be frozen and kept in 'sperm banks' for use at a later date, and the new 'high tech' procedures IVF (in vitro fertilisation) and GIFT (gamete intrafallopian transfer) used to assist otherwise infertile women to conceive may in some cases also involve donor gametes. But in most infertility programmes donors are guaranteed anonymity, and as with adoption, the true identity of the people created is concealed.

In the words of New Zealand's Adoption Support Link director Anna Coffey: 'As adoption has done in the past, new birth technologies, in different ways and degrees, represent a potent threat to the sense of biological identity.

'In adoption, the "secrecy is best" view was widely promoted by professionals involved in the process. To some extent we have seen doctors maintain the same view of AID identity . . . it is now well documented that adults with AID conceptions are seeking their origins just as adopted people have done before them (British Agencies for Adoption and Fostering medical group AID working party, 1984).

'Successful parenting does not depend on a biological connection; it is based on trust, honesty, love and mutual self-respect. Children of the new birth technologies have an equal right to be told the truth and to have access to information about themselves. To legally sanction the deception of a child on a matter so intrinsically important to psychological functioning is an abuse of law, no less in AID than it once was in the case of adoption. Issuing fictional birth certificates will not dispose of the human need for identity.'

Anna Coffey adds that to her knowledge, only Sweden has legislated for information to be made available for people (eighteen years and over) conceived through AID.

In the United States sperm banks are booming business, not only because of infertility, but also because frozen sperm can be guaranteed AIDS-free (Acquired Immune Deficiency Syndrome) through time-delay testing of donors, and as 'fertility insurance' for couples who feel they may not be able to conceive in the future, either through the man's death or later sterility. In an article about the popularity of sperm banks in California (*Dominion*, January 1988) British journalist Ivor Davis, based in Los Angeles, also considered the products created: the people.

'The most famous of them, and by far the most vocal, has been Suzanne Rubin, a Los Angeles teacher who found out when she was thirty-two that the man she had called father all her life was not, and that on one side, her ancestry came from a frozen file in a nitrogen tank.

'It produced in her a rage which sent her on a campaign to find the anonymous medical student who had given her life. By a tortuous process of elimination she found out that her actual father was one of fifty-five Jewish medical students at the University of Southern California in the fifties.

'Geneticists at the university told her he would have had blue eyes and either red hair or have relatives with red hair. That narrowed it down to ten.

'She didn't expect to like him much, when and if she found him.

' "What kind of man drops off his sperm, collects $25 for it and then walks off with no thought of responsibility?" she said bitterly. "I don't hate him but I have a tough time saying my father sold me for that amount." '

Davis also reported: 'Besides the moral objections, artificial insemination by sperm bank donor is still a subject in many places stuck in a legal quagmire. Legislation simply has not been able to keep up with the spiralling technology.

'Some states still have regulations which absolve the donors of responsibility and make the father on record the legal father as well. Some states still rule the children of artificial insemination to be illegitimate.

'Husbands have sued wives for adultery because they became pregnant by insemination. In one famous case, a couple who conceived their child by artificial insemination separated and when the husband requested visitation rights, the wife argued he had no such rights because he wasn't the child's natural father.

'. . . [Some] doctors pore over studies of probability and have cut down drastically on the number of inseminations from each donor's sperm since *Time* magazine reported that a marriage had to be prevented at the last moment in New York, because the bride and groom were found to have both resulted from the same donor father.'

New Zealand legislation to cover new birth technologies and the status of the people conceived through it was still being considered at the time of writing.

Conclusion

With new issues within adoption and related areas arising, lobby groups are also becoming more outspoken and the issues which appear most likely to come under public scrutiny in the foreseeable future include:

The rights of infertile people to methods of obtaining children.

The promotion of open adoption an alternative to abortion.

The promotion of guardianship in place of adoption as a means of caring for children unable to be parented by their natural parents.

When, or if, these questions gain greater prominence, it must be remembered that adoption should never again be the only option open to women who feel they are unable to bring up their children, and more importantly, that for whatever reason natural parents are unable to care for their children, either on a temporary or long-term basis, the emotional and physical wellbeing of the children concerned must be paramount in all situations.

APPENDICES

Adult Adoption Information Act: facts and figures

The Adult Adoption Information Act, passed on 11 September 1985, and which came into full force on 1 September 1986, has opened the doors for the estimated 50,000 New Zealand-born adults who were adopted by strangers and their birth parents to make contact with each other. There are estimated to be a total of about 100,000 adoptees (through both stranger and non-stranger adoptions) in New Zealand — about 3.1 per cent of the total population.

The Act allows adult adoptees (twenty years and over) access to their full original birth certificate unless a ten-year renewable veto on identifying information has been placed by the birth parent or parents named on the certificate. If there is no veto, the certificate will, in most instances, provide the adoptee's original name, birth mother's name, age and birthplace. In many cases the place for the father's name simply states: 'No Details Recorded'. The legislation requires adoptees to undergo compulsory counselling — either in person or by telephone — with an approved counsellor (of whom not all are Social Welfare Department staff) before the certificate is handed over. However, the counsellor cannot withhold the certificate if the adoptee is unco-operative during the counselling. If a veto has been placed, the certificate will be sent directly to the adoptee, but with details of the birth parent or parents omitted. It will show the adoptee's place of birth, date of birth, sex and original first names if any were given.

The Act also allows birth parents (named on the original birth certificate) the right to seek contact with the daughter or son they relinquished for adoption, providing the adoptee is twenty years or older. If the adoptee has not placed a veto, the Social Welfare Department will endeavour to trace her or him on behalf of the birth parent and ask if she or he wishes to be identified.

If so, the department will pass on the adoptee's name and address to the birth parent. If not, or if the adoptee has placed a veto, no identifying information will be made available to the birth parent. In cases where there is no veto but the department is unable to locate the adoptee, her or his name will be made available to the birth parent.

Both adoptees and birth parents have been able to place vetoes — either by letter or telephone — since March 1986, and in the six months leading up to the time when the new legislation became fully active, 653 adoptees (nineteen years and over), and 2243 birth parents (with daughters or sons nineteen years and over) placed vetoes. A veto expires after ten years, and can be renewed or revoked at any time.

In the first year that adoptees and birth parents had the right to officially seek contact with each other, 5834 adult adoptees received their original birth certificate and 1128 birth parents requested the department trace their daughter or son. A further 2000 to 3000 birth mothers also asked the Social Welfare Department to record that should their daughter or son want to locate them, they would be happy for that to occur. Department Assistant Director for Adoption and Fostering from 1978 to 1987, Ann Corcoran, estimates that about ninety per cent of the adoptees and birth parents who have used the Act have made contact with each other, and adds that there is no evidence to suggest most contacts are not successful or that those concerned regret it. (At the time of writing no research had been conducted in this area, though research is planned by the department — subject to resources.) She also says that the percentage of adoptees applying for their original birth certificates is surprisingly high when compared with other countries where identifying information is available. No comparisons can be made in the birth parent applications because New Zealand is the only country in the world where legislation has been passed to allow them access to identifying information.

Prior to the Adult Adoption Information Act it was not illegal for adoptees and birth parents to trace each other, but the secrecy laws meant it was often a lengthy and difficult search. In some cases adoptees were able to get enough identifying inform-

ation from their adoptive parents on which to base a search —
if the parents knew the birth mother's name, which wasn't the
case in all situations. And there were some Social Welfare
Department staff and hospital staff who were sympathetic and
prepared to bend the rules. But Keith Griffith, active in the cause
for opening records and author of 'Adoption — Procedures —
Documentation — Statistics — New Zealand 1881–1981', estimated that only one in twenty-five adoptees who attempted to
trace their birth mother would be successful. Adoptees could
apply to the courts for information on special grounds, but while
the interpretation of 'special grounds' did become more liberal,
the first decision to release information was made in October
1978, and since that time only about fifty cases are known to
have been successful. (Mary Iwanek, SWD, 1987.)

Adoption groups were formed in some areas to provide emotional and practical support for adoptees and birth relatives
seeking contact with each other, and to lobby for changes in
legislation. The best known of the groups is Jigsaw, formed in
Auckland in 1976, which began a contact register for adoptees
and birth mothers who wished to meet. But the register was
dependent on both sides joining the organisation and paying
their membership fees. (The Jigsaw register is still operating but
now deals mainly with cases where the adoptee is under twenty.)

But despite growing support for access to information, the
Adult Adoption Information Act was not passed without a
lengthy battle. Labour MP for New Lynn (Auckland) since 1966,
Jonathan Hunt, who was neither personally nor professionally
involved in adoption, took up the fight in the late 1970s following
requests from some of his constituents. Hunt, in Opposition at
the time, began what became a series of Private Member's Bills
designed to open access to adoption records, each one failing to
make progress. By 1984 his latest attempt looked promising, but
a snap election in July that year meant every Bill before the
House lapsed. However, while there had been a great deal of
opposition to the proposed legislation from the National Government, particularly from then Prime Minister Sir Robert Muldoon,
there was strong support from Labour MPs — and Labour won
the election. Hunt was appointed Minister of Broadcasting and

Postmaster-General, and therefore was unable to introduce Private Member's Bills and handed over his adoption Bill to Wellington Central MP since 1982, Fran Wilde, also an adoptive mother. The Bill proceeded quickly from that point and on the night of 11 September 1985 was passed on a conscience vote of fifty-one to twenty-five.

Three years later both Hunt and Wilde say they would have personally preferred the final Bill not to contain such a strong veto clause, but that without the clause it would have been unlikely to have been passed.

Wilde looks at it in this way: 'My personal preference in fact would be no veto, but politically I don't think we would have got it through without that . . . my personal reply [to the lobby for veto provisions] is that the need of the adoptee is actually paramount. I understand people's feelings, and I suppose there are a lot of older women in particular who would be pretty scared — but I have seen so many people [adoptees] so obsessive about who they are that it's taken over their whole being. They don't actually want to go round and say, "Hello, Mum!" They don't actually want to go round and break into their birth mothers' lives and wreck their marriages. They are quite sensitive about that but they desperately want to be able to place themselves somewhere. And also, all the literature I have read from overseas indicates that the negative factors are absolutely minimal — and in the end when you are making laws you must cater for what is in fact the overwhelming majority, and I think the need there is great.'

Hunt, though personally preferring a less strong veto clause and the 'adult' age set at eighteen rather than twenty, is happy with the Act as it stands and says: 'The advantage of it going through all those times, and there was one advantage, was that we got the Bill refined and we got it right.'

History of adoption legislation in New Zealand

1881: The Adoption of Children Act 1881, introduced as a Private Member's Bill, was the first adoption legislation in New Zealand. Its principal purpose was to give some security to the adoptive parent and child as prior to this adoption had been a rather informal process. Nothing in the Act limited access to birth records.

1915: The Births and Deaths Registration Amendment Act 1915 provided for adoptees' births to be re-registered with the new adoptive details replacing the originals — apparently to protect the adoptee from the stigma of illegitimacy. Issuing of the original birth certificate was restricted to certified purposes, though anyone could still inspect it.

1924: The Births and Deaths Registration Act 1924 made it a little more difficult to obtain a copy of the original certificate but did not restrict inspection.

1951: The Births and Deaths Registration Amendment Act 1951 applied the restriction in the 1915 and 1924 Acts to the inspection of the records as well as the supply of copies. Access was at the discretion of the registrar or Registrar General. As with the 1924 Act, records of parliamentary debate are not helpful on the reasons for this change.

1955: The Adoption Act 1955 allowed a birth parent to give consent to an adoption without knowing the identity of the adoptive parents. The Act also limited access to 'adoption records', though it is unclear why. The interdepartmental committee's report, on which the Act was based, included the recommendation 'that a Judge's or a Magistrate's order be required for the production or inspection of adoption records and then only on special grounds . . . the committee thinks that the records should be regarded as absolutely confidential and not disclosed to anyone except in particular circumstances'.

1961: The Births and Deaths Registration Amendment Act 1961 provided for adoptees' birth certificates to be the same as for non-adopted people.

1969: The Births and Deaths Registration Amendment 1969 closed off to an even greater extent access to original birth certificates. In effect, it prevented the Registrar General from releasing information where to do so would contravene the principles of the Adoption Act.

1985: The Adult Adoption Information Act was passed.

Overseas background

Scotland: Since 1930 all adoptees seventeen years and over had had access of right to their original birth certificate. In 1972 and again in 1980 the Registrar General of Scotland reported that there had been no complaints about the working of the system.

England: Since 1975 all adoptees eighteen years and over have had access of right, after at least one counselling session, to their original birth certificate. In 1980 the Registrar General's Office, responding to questions of privacy invasion, said it had not received any complaints of actual privacy invasion, but had received several letters fearing it.

USA: Each of the states have their own adoption statutes, with only a handful of states allowing open access to records.

Finland: Since 1925 all adoptees, adoptive parents and birth parents have had access to both the original and current birth certificates of the adoptee. Access is not provided in the Finnish Adoption Act but is part of Finnish law — all court documents are available to any person who is party to any action.

Israel: Since 1960 all adoptees aged eighteen and over have access of right to their original birth certificate subject to counselling and a waiting period of forty-five days from date of application.

Holland: Since 1956 all adoptees may have access to their original birth certificate at any time. From the age of twelve the adoptee or adoptive parents have access to the adoption records.

Australia (as of October 1987):

A.C.T.: No access to original birth certificate.
  No contact register.
  Non-identifying information available to adoptees and relin-
quishing mothers.
  Legislation under review.

New South Wales: No access to original birth certificate.
  State-run contact register.
  Non-identifying information available to adult adoptees and
relinquishing parents.
  Legislation under review.

Northern Territory: No access to original birth certificate.
  State-run contact register.
  Non-identifying information available from about 1962 for
adoptees and relinquishing mothers.
  Legislation under review.

Queensland: No access to original birth certificate.
  State-run contact register (requires registration from adoptee,
birth parents and adoptive parents).
  Jigsaw contact register (registration by adoptive parents not
required).
  Non-identifying information available to adoptees and relinquishing mothers.

South Australia: No access to original birth certificate.
  State-run contact register.
  Non-identifying information available to adoptees and relin-
quishing mothers.
  Legislation under review — seems likely that adoptees over
eighteen will have access to original birth certificate.

Tasmania: No access to original birth certificate.
  Jigsaw contact register.
  Non-identifying information available for adult adoptees and
relinquishing mothers.
  Legislation under review.

Victoria: Adult adoptees (over eighteen) entitled, after counselling, to original birth certificate and/or non-identifying information.

Birth parents entitled to up-to-date non-identifying information. If the adult adoptee agrees, identifying information can be given or a meeting arranged. (However, the current waiting list is understood to be seven years!)

State-run contact register.

Western Australia: Adult adoptees (over eighteen) have access to original birth certificate after compulsory counselling unless birth parent/s have placed a veto requesting no contact.

State-run contact register.

MORE ABOUT PENGUINS

For further information about books available from Penguin please write to the following:

In New Zealand: For a complete list of books available from Penguin in New Zealand write to the Marketing Department, Penguin Books (N.Z.) Ltd, Private Bag, Takapuna, Auckland.

In Australia: For a complete list of books available from Penguin in Australia write to the Marketing Department, Penguin Books Australia Ltd, P.O. Box 257, Ringwood, Victoria 3134.

In Britain: For a complete list of books available from Penguin in Britain write to Dept EP, Penguin Books Ltd, Harmondsworth, Middlesex UB7 0DA.

In the U.S.A.: For a complete list of books available from Penguin in the United States write to Dept DG, Penguin Books, 299 Murray Hill Parkway, East Rutherford, New Jersey 07073.

In Canada: For a complete list of books available from Penguin in Canada write to Penguin Books Canada Ltd, 2801 John Street, Markham, Ontario L3R 1B4.